"UP OUR LOBBY"

by
Bill Houldin

REMINISCENCES OF LIFE IN THE DOCK COTTAGES BIRKENHEAD BETWEEN 1915-1938

Published by:
Birkenhead Central Library, Department of Leisure Services
& Tourism, Wirral Borough Council.

ISBN 0 904582 08 6

This Booklet is dedicated to Joe & Ann Houldin, without whom nothing
would have been possible.

LOCAL REMINISCENCE SERIES

This is the first in what is is hoped will be a series of reminiscences by local people,
published by Birkenhead Central Library.
Bill Houldin lived in the "Dock Cottages" from 1915 to 1933 and this narrative
describes life as he saw it in what were probably the first blocks of flats in England.

Chapter 1
"BUILDING BLOCKS"

The Dock Cottages, on rare occasions referred to as the "Queens Buildings", but more generally spoken of as "The Blocks", were built to accommodate the workers who were to build the Birkenhead dock system in the mid 1800s.

Expert opinion and comments on the project were wide and varied. Some were loud with praise, others just as vociferous in condemnation, before the plans finally materialised into bricks and mortar.

An interesting set of plans in miniature was presented to the readers of the "Liverpool Journal", on May 3rd, 1845. The heading was as follows:—

"PLANS, ELEVATIONS AND SECTIONS OF FIREPROOF DWELLINGS FOR THE WORKMEN OF BIRKENHEAD DOCK COMPANY, NOW IN PROCESS OF ERECTION AT BIRKENHEAD."

A feature of this plan was that eight roads were shown converging on what was to be St. James Church. One, to be called Vyner Street, never materialised. The remaining seven roads, with one exception, were named as on the plan. They were Corporation, Sumner, Tollemache, Stanley and Ilchester Roads, plus Laird Street. The exception, not named on the plan as such but as a continuation of Corporation Road, became Hoylake Road.

The fact that eight roads were envisaged but only seven emerged was very intriguing to me, because old Ellen Purcell, of whom more in another chapter, always claimed that her father, who farmed the area long before this project was thought of, had told his children of an old prophecy which was, that the land upon which St. James Church was later to be built would be the meeting place at some future date for seven lane ends. Within Ellen's time this "prophecy" became fact, not lane ends, but great road ends culminating in a church roundabout.

This scheme was something entirely new in England. It was sometimes referred to as "the Edinburgh plan" having its origins in dwellings such as existed in that city. This new project in housing aroused nationwide interest. So much indeed, that eminent architects and planners were sent by various bodies and authorities to view the Dock Cottages and to report back from, as Dr. Quentin Hughes, Reader in Architecture put it : "Birkenhead, this city of innovation."

The narration accompanying the "Liverpool Journal" plan stated that —

"The directors of the Birkenhead Dock Company, finding that they must provide accommodation for the numerous workmen required for the construction of their warehouses and docks, or submit to the great inconvenience, expense and delay in consequence of the want of it, have determined to erect a number of dwellings for their labourers and mechanics.

After calculating the cost of all returns from various descriptions of cottages submitted to them, they have decided to build to the accompanying plans designed by C.E. Lang Esq., considering that by their adoption, the greatest amount of comfort will be afforded to the occupiers that can be combined with a fair return upon the capital invested. Each dwelling will have an unlimited supply of water, a gas light, and all rates and taxes will be paid by the company. The tenant to pay in one fixed sum per week, all charges incident to the occupation of the dwelling."

Signed MacGregor Laird, (Secretary).

The plan shows St. James Church, which was endowed and in process of erection at the cost of its benefactors, William Potter, William Jackson and John and MacGregor Laird, and was designed to accommodate 1,000 persons.

Also on the plan, at the apex of the triangle of land which was to contain "A" Block, and directly opposite to the projected church, is shown a space earmarked for a school to take 500 pupils. The space was never used for this purpose.

Another non-starter on the plan was a parsonage house. This building was intended to stand on a plot which was between the roads which became Hoylake and Stanley Roads.

As stated there was a divergence of opinion among the experts as to the merits or otherwise of this new concept in building. There follows a synopsis of those opposing views.

Quote from Chambers Journal, February 1847.

Among the best homes brought into operation in regard to erecting new houses, is that at Birkenhead, the rising town opposite Liverpool. Some time ago the 'Times' presented an account of the visit of Mr. Chadwick and gentlemen to the dwellings erected for the working classes, from which we gather the following particulars — "Without drawings or plans, it would be difficult to give an accurate conception of the improvements. The buildings are four-storeyed, of red brick, with light sandstone window sills and copings. Their external aspect would suggest to the Londoner the idea of a block of buildings constructed for professional persons for an Inn of Court of Chancery and with little addition and variation of ornament, they might match with the new hall of Lincolns Inn. They are, in fact, flats or sets of chambers, consisting of two sets on each floor. Each set consists of one living room and two sleeping rooms. The floors are of arched bricks. The living room is floored with a hard, Welsh fire brick tile. The sleeping room floors are boarded. The staircases are of stone, with iron balustrades. The flat brick arches, of which the floors are constructed, are tied together with iron ties, and the whole building is fireproof. The most important points of improvement are, however, those in which principles of the sanitary report, in respect to the means of cleansing and ventilation for the working classes, are carried out. Each set of rooms is furnished with a constant supply of water, and also sinks for washing, and a water closet, and means of communication with a dust shaft from the whole set of chambers by which all dust and ashes might be removed at once from the apartments without the necessity of the inmates leaving them. The party entered the rooms which were inhabited and questioned the inhabitants as to their experience of them. One nursing mother, in a neat and well kept set of rooms, attested to the superior convenience of this arrangement as a most important relief from the fatigue and exposure to the weather in a common town dwelling. She had now no occasion to leave her child alone while she went to a distance to fetch water, neither had she to keep dirty or waste water or dirt and ashes in the room until she could find time to carry them away. She had "now scarcely ever to go downstairs and leave her child."

Each set of rooms is provided with one conduit for the ingress of fresh air, and another for the egress of vitiated air. Those examined were newly inhabited but the immediate sanitary effect of the arrangements was perceptible to those who have visited such abodes, in the absence of offensive effluvia or of those smells. This observation was extended to the whole range of buildings. The sinks in each room were trapped with "Bell traps" as were all the openings to the drains and gully shoots in the paved courts and thoroughfares. A constant supply of water was secured. The house drains were well flushed with water and cesspools were entirely abolished. This range of buildings is perhaps the first practical example of the entire removal of one chief source of physical depression and pestilence common to all existing dwellings of the working classes in towns. The price at which these objects were attained was the next topic of enquiry. The rents charged were from 3/- to 5/- each, according to position. This included a constant supply of water and the use of one gas burner in each set of rooms, and all rates and taxes and, moreover, two iron bedsteads, with an oven and convenient fixtures."

Letter to the "Liverpool Mercury" — Friday, May 28th 1847.
"Scotch" plan of living in flats. A remedy for narrow streets and courts.

Gentlemen, I recommend the council to get power from parliament to build a few streets in the Scotch plan of flats. That is, because seven or eight storeys high with room for one or more families on each floor. The advantages are — the ground floor would be made the most of. The poorer the family the higher and more airy would be the room it occupied. The streets might be wider. The town would have a more stately and city like air, even in its poorer quarters. I think if the example were once set by the corporation, the private builders would follow it. (J.H.)

Editor's reply to the above.
We confess we do not like the Scotch plan of living in flats, separate families occupying distinct storeys, all having access by one alpine staircase. The subject however, is worthy of discussion after the experience which has been had in Edinburgh and Glasgow.

Unknown Traveller's Description
Birkenhead is entered from Wallasey at Wallasey Pool, crossing at a point presenting unusual claims to attention. In the road leading from the bridge are immense piles of lofty buildings bearing the rather inappropriate name of the "Dock Cottages". These buildings do not seem to meet the approval of the class of persons for whom they were intended: only about a dozen of them are as yet inhabited, and even these have changed their tenants several times. Their mode of construction has been the subject of much diversity of opinion, but unquestionably their distance, according to the present arrangements, from the proposed Graving docks will render them very inconvenient for the labourers and others employed at these works. It is calculated that these houses will furnish residences for about sixteen hundred persons, for whose accommodation the elegant church of St. James, which forms the great architectural ornament of the neighbourhood, has been erected. The land between the Poulton bridge and this church belongs to The Birkenhead Dock Company, whose property extends from hence to the Woodside Ferry, a distance of two miles, by the margin of Wallasey Pool, a creek which for ages has only served to absorb a portion of the tidal waters, leaving at the reflux of every tide, some hundred acres of barren weed, exhaling noxious vapours by which the surrounding atmosphere was infected.

The foundation of the docks was laid on 23rd October 1844 by Sir Philip de Malpas Grey Egerton: Bart.

Report from an unidentified source. 1847.
Every facility should be afforded for erecting healthier cottages for the working classes and for putting a stop to the habit of crowding large numbers into a small space. We are sorry however, to see very little, if any, progression in the plans for erecting cottage houses. We had read a good deal about an improved system of building cottages at Birkenhead, and were given to understand that these cottages were looked upon as models. Last week we took an opportunity of inspecting them, but we confess we were bitterly disappointed. Instead of convenient and roomy cottages with yards or little gardens attached, and situated in wide airy streets, we found that these "Improved cottages" 350 in number, were built in streets only 6 yards wide with a cross street at the end preventing all circulation; that the tenements were piled one on top of the other in "Flats" after the Edinburgh fashion, and that none had a single inch of outdoor yard, either back or front. The buildings are four storeys high with a common stair for every eight families who are to live one above another. The apartments also are wretchedly

small, measuring only 13' x 9'9" and two bedrooms each measuring 9' x 6'. As the wives sometimes say "There is not room to whip a cat in them." As to the health of the people who live in such narrow streets, pent up at one end, and crowded in in vast numbers, it is unnecessary to remark, let fever break out and the scourge would be dreadful.

Each of these cottages is to have a dust hole, down which all the refuse will descend into one common receptacle; gas light, water tap and water closet. These, although conveniences, cannot compensate for want of room and want of ventilation. The roofs are surrounded by a battlement and the clothes will be dried on the tops of the houses. The cottages are erected by the Dock Company and are intended for their labourers, and we think that no one would occupy them from choice. Most likely the poor families, depending upon the Dock Company for employment for subsistence, will be obliged to become unwilling tenants. The altitude of the buildings, the narrowness of the streets, the prominent and peculiar appearance of the narrow, closed windows, and the uniformity of the whole range, gives the pile of buildings, at a distance, the appearance of a large hospital or asylum or barracks. They are built remote from the town and about two miles from the ferry, a situation, we presume, where the price of the land could be an object. "We were most disappointed."

Chapter 2
EARLY REMINISCENCES

"The Blocks" — two small words which conjure up a multitude of memories for so many people, some old, some not so old. All will have passed down through generations, anecdotes, more than likely embellished with the passage of time, all with a degree of nostalgia, which only a person born in this unique collection of dwellings would appreciate.

The Dock Cottages were unique in that they were the first "flats" in England. However, it is the remarkable families and individuals who breathed life into the bricks and mortar whose life pattern and achievements will long be remembered.

Neighbour, in its context of the people next door, or in the same street, had no place in our vocabulary. Our next door neighbours, or even people up the same lobby were virtually of each other's family. To a slightly lesser degree the same relationship applied to the whole block in which we lived. Loyalties therefore ran in order of — family, lobby, block and collectively "The Blocks" in slightly diminishing order. As the three musketeers were "Each for all, all for one", so the Dock Cottagers were "One family for 350, 350 families for one."

The blocks have produced an abundance of personalities from Alderman and Town Mayor, through golf, football and boxing champions, to healers, humorists and amateur philosophers.

It was literally true that every contingency from the cradle to the grave was covered by someone, or something, in this seething pool of humanity which constituted the heart of the blocks.

At birth, if Nurse Davies or Granny Sherlock were otherwise engaged, there were a dozen or so amateur midwives ready, willing and able to bring one or more new "Blockite" into the world.

Likewise with illness, and we experienced overall, every conceivable disease from measles, scarlet fever, dipheria etc. to T.B., a host of 'specialists' would be forthcoming. If a parent was stricken then the children could be assured of succour from a dozen surrogate mothers.

In the event of the ultimate tragedy occuring, the bereaved were not given the chance or time to suffer one degree more than was absolutely necessary. All was taken care of even to the "laying out". Each block was able to produce at least one person especially adept at this unenviable task.

The blocks mothers were a breed of their own, passing down, mother to daughter, some indefinable quality of understanding and humanitarianism so sadly lacking today.

As a child one could, and did, run to the nearest mother for a scrape to be kissed or a consoling pat to be administered to a bumped head. Nor was it a problem to find such sympathetic treatment. Out of the three lobbies comprising the block there would be a small group of three or four women standing talking at one or more lobby bottom.

Smaller children were allowed to stand with their own mother's group. You would then be privy to all the secrets of women's talk, albeit in ignorance of the sense of it. However, on occasion, for reasons by then not entirely unknown to you, you would be despatched with a smart clip across the ear and an admonishing "Push off, big ears."

The nearest parallel to be drawn to today's society and our women's lobbies groups, would be the present day ladies coffee mornings, the great difference being the topics of conversation. The lobbies group would be their children and survival, this whilst standing close together, arms folded across the chest and "pinafore" wrapped over folded arms in a manner strangely characteristic of the women of our class and period.

The words covetousness or envy never entered our world because the standard of living throughout the blocks was on par. You could not begrudge someone something they did not possess. If you did not work you did not eat. You certainly cut back or cut out drinking and smoking. If your stamped card contained the requisite number you drew dole. When you were ineligible for dole you were obliged to seek assistance from the Board of Guardians. As this hand out was just a pittance, certainly not enough to sustain an average family, many of our neighbours were in dire straits.

Fortunately my family were never hungry. My parents always managed, unemployed or otherwise, to keep the family fed and clothed.

I must confess however to partaking in what was common practice on more than one occasion. The local boys used to stand around the dock area, notably Ranks Flour Mills and the Vacuum Oil Co., waiting for the workmen to come out. The cry then would be "Any bread left, Mister?" We could rely on at least one left over sandwich at each stint.

What the consequences of my being caught "begging" would have been had my parents known, does not bear thinking about. Family pride was very high on the Houldin list, as it was with the majority of our neighbours.

THE HOULDINS

I first saw the light of day on 17th October 1915 at 31 G Block, the youngest of five children; Ann, Louisa (Lou), Julia (May). Three loving, devoted sisters who thoroughly spoiled me. Brother Joe, although I am positive was just as devoted, quite naturally kept me in my place in the manner of all elder brothers.

This wonderful language of ours does not contain enough superlatives to adequately describe the bond between us as brothers and sisters, or for the love bestowed upon us by our beloved parents.

Ann Kelly and little Joe Houldin, all 5'4" of him, were meant for each other. We, in turn, were blessed, as no other children were blessed, to be born to such parents.

Mother

My mother was the eldest child of one William Patrick Kelly. He was a Flour Mill Warehouse manager for Vernons in Liverpool where she was born. The Houldin family did not exist as far as he was concerned.

My maternal grandmother was an elegant, beautiful lady. This I know from a photograph still in my possession. I was never privileged to see her in person, she having died before I was born.

The reason for my mother's estrangement from her father was one John Joseph Houldin, of Wallasey, a little man who, in his youth, carted coal, bricks, etc. with a horse drawn cart. In his spare time and during periods of unemployment, he would accept challenges from travelling boxing booth pugilists for a few shillings. He eventually became a professional boxer appearing frequently at the old Liverpool Stadium, Pudsey Street. A further minus factor was that he was a Protestant, non-practicing.

The Kelly family had by now moved across the river to Seacombe. Grandfather having transferred to a similar job at Vernons Mill on the Wallasey dock side.

I suppose it must have been written in the stars, or some other such romantic idea, that Annie Kelly, who by this time was courting, and word has it, almost affianced to a Jeweller/Pawnbroker's son, should meet my father. The Jeweller's shop has long gone, but the Jeweller's name is immortalized in the fact that the corner upon which it stood was, and still is, known as "Lloyd's corner."

It is almost certain that Grandfather Kelly's disapproval of his daughter's choice of a mate — a carter, boxer and protestant, — was the reason why he cut her off and we never did know him.

My one and only meeting with him was at my uncle's wedding. Even at this event I understand he did not speak to my mother, although I was too young to know these things.

The estrangement manifested itself during the depression in the thirties. Things were getting desperate in our household. So much so that I recall the agonising decision made by my parents to swallow their pride and send my brother across the docks to Vernons Mill to enquire whether my grandfather would provide a job for the boy. To his eternal shame the answer given was a definite "No". This, without a word of sympathy for the family's plight. Fortunes changed but the memory lingers on.

Dad

Dad, although small, packed a punch like a heavyweight. His boxing experiences covered everything from fairground boxing booths, where five shillings was the prize if one could last three rounds with the booth boxer, to the Liverpool Stadium, where he boxed and beat many well known names of the day. I have been informed by many of his contemporaries who saw him box that the fact that he was virtually unmarked facially, was due to his outstanding defensive prowess, particularly when his back was to the ropes. Mother often referred to his "rope burns" across his shoulders.

On rare occasions, when some outside occurrence had really upset him, the family would sit and silently witness his frustration. It is a strange fact of life that there is a section of society which feels that its function is to incite ex boxers to strike when taunted. Dad would come home after such a confrontation and would pace the floor and on more than one occasion, punch a panel out of a door.

I was twenty and boxing myself when I remembered these panel-punching episodes. I was actually working in a door factory and asked a labourer to hold a door while I tried to emulate Dad's panel trick. The result was catastrophic. I had stupidly forgotten that panels in father's day were in $\frac{1}{4}$" thick wood, whilst modern panels, one of which I was about to attack, are made of 3-ply wood — almost impossible to demolish, even with a large hammer. The result of this experiment was a fist rapidly changing to a lovely shade of purple, and a badly sprained wrist — a very painful lesson indeed.

When Dad gave up boxing he had two main interests. One was as trainer to Wirral Railway F.C., the other to have my brother, Joe, follow in his boxing footsteps. I was too young to be aware of the details, but the facts, as they have been related to me regarding his plans for Joe, are that he used to train my brother, and another boy called John Saddler, also a "Blocks" boy. They were of similar size, weight and both ten years old. I understand they were about on par in ability.

In those days most towns had fairly regular carnival or Fete days when all manner of sporting events and amusements were indulged in. Dad would take the "Houldin twins", as they were billed, to box exhibitions at these events.

Brother Joe became very proficient at the game and a bright future as a boxer was envisaged for him. Unfortunately, as he grew older, his enthusiasm waned, and other pursuits, notably dancing, took his fancy. It was apparent, even to me at my age, that this was a great disappointment to my father. My own inclination and abilities lay with football but love for my father and awareness of his disappointment, drove me to join the "Conway" Boxing Club with my workmate "Ginger" Griffiths, in the hope that I might, in some small measure, compensate for his loss. My name did appear on half a dozen or so Bills, mainly at Birkenhead Stadium over "Herons" Garage, Park Entrance, now "Dutton Forshaws", alas never more than as a lowly 6-rounder. For this I was paid 12/6d for a win and 10/- if unsuccessful.

Long after his Wirral Railway days, indeed almost until he died in his seventies, Dad held open house on Sundays for anyone needing physio. treatment. Many well known local sportsmen took advantage of Dad's skill as a masseur, when his untrained, but very skilled fingers, would knead away aches and bruises acquired by these "patients" from the football field or from the ring. Ever since nis death I have had the pleasure of listening to men testifying to the efficaciousness of little Joe's home-made embrocation and massage techniques.

Although love was the predominant feature in our lives, we were obliged to adhere rigidly to a code of conduct which brooked no deviation from the straight and narrow. This code of conduct was not the prerogative of our family. The same could be said of the majority of Blocks people. In spite of the fact that the lobbies were not lit at all. If one lived at the top, four flights of stone steps had to be negotiated in pitch darkness before reaching the door. Young or old, male or female, there was never any question of molestation, physically, or even verbally. Respect for persons and property was paramount.

Each flight of stone steps was the unwritten responsibility of the pair of mothers at each level. The cleaning was done, not by any sophisticated machine, but by primitive soap, scrubbing brushes and sheer physical effort on hands and knees. A feature of this weekly operation was that after scrubbing, each step edge would be rubbed with "Donkey Stone" to about 2 inches back. This would leave a greyish edge to the step making a very pleasing finish.

My own recollections of the Blocks is that of dwellings, four storeys high, in parallel lines plus one vertical to the others. The term "flats" was never used, the word being unknown, as the Dock Cottages were the first of their type in England.

Our own Block "G" was, of course, the hub of our own little world, each family knowing each other's members to the point of intimacy. Up our own lobby we had the Ellisons, the Wally Thoms, Tates, Sis and Tom Atherton and family, old Mrs. Tears, Nell Noonan and family, the Threlfalls and the Ashleys.

The next lobby housed, among others, Jim Atherton and his family. Others in our block were the Knowles/Griffiths, Bullocks, Rose Ann, Annie and Jimmy Doyle, Meggitts and Newtons and many others.

The "Avenues" or "passages" marked on the plans were never referred to as such. The collective term "The Blocks" was used to describe the buildings, the spaces, streets or passages, call them what you will, in between. These were 18 feet wide, wall to wall, with gas lamps bracketed to the walls at intervals of about 30 feet and 18 feet from ground level.

Our lamp lighter, "Ted Cheers", was an integral part of Dock Cottage life. He would appear just before sunset, a long bamboo pole over his shoulder. At the end of the pole was an attachment which was used to push up a small trap door in the base of the lamp. A hook next to the push attachment, was engaged in a ring which, when pulled down, fired the incandescent mantle. At sunrise the process would be reversed.

The living room, or kitchen as we called it, was 13 feet by 9 feet and 8 feet 6 inches high. Two bedrooms 9 feet x 8 feet six inches led directly from the kitchen. Privacy therefore was almost non-existent.

Heating was provided by a coal fire in the kitchen. Built into the fireplace was an oven. The whole unit, fire bars, oven top and doors were always black-leaded and polished mirror-like. Nearly every home possessed a set of fire irons, fender, pokers, tongs, shovel and a variety of ornaments, all emery-papered until they shone like silver. My family graduated to a set of brass "fire irons" which my father polished every week-end. I am now the proud owner of these brasses which I endeavour to maintain as did my father.

The only light for all rooms was provided by one gas lamp fixed to the wall in the kitchen, generally over, and to the right of, the fire. As in the street lamps, an incandescent mantle was used. So fragile were those mantles that they could be broken simply by removing them from the box when new. After hours of use the risk was multiplied a dozen fold. Mothers usually managed to produce an attractive shade, mainly in glass, to enhance this very dull light.

The back kitchen, which also led directly from the kitchen but on the opposite side from the bedroom, was barely five feet wide, most of the space being taken up by a heavy sandstone sink roughly 3 feet 6 inches by 2 feet by 8 inches deep, serviced by a cold water tap only. This space also served as our ablution area, real baths being taken in a tin bath and in front of the fire when possible.

The lavatory was reached through another door from the back kitchen. To use the word "toilet" would be to bestow far too much dignity on what was simply a brick cubicle with a boarded box set against the outer wall. In the centre of the box was an appropriately-shaped hole. When ones bodily functions were performed it was an easy step or two to the tap at the sink to fill the ever present bucket and to hurl the water with as much force as one could muster, into the hole. The more force used the quicker the waste would be forced-down the outlet pipe, a far cry from the present day luxury of a siphon cistern.

In the same lavatory space, and set into the wall facing the door, was a steel hinged plate about 2 feet square. This plate concealed a hole into which was fed all household waste. The chute was common to the four dwellings in that line of descent. The discarded waste from all four eventually found its way to, what is described on the plan as a "Dust Cellar". To the occupants these were known as "middens".

The "midden" or cellar was below ground level and access to it from outside was by two flap doors which, when pulled open from the middle, exposed the contents within.

The "muck" cart arrived at infrequent intervals to relieve us of our waste. These cellars, the contents of which was rotting matter, vegetables, bones, ashes etc. inevitably became the breeding ground for rats. Just as inevitably, with the rats we had dogs which were famous as "ratters". On many occasions the midden doors were lifted between the dust carts calls to give the ratters some practice.

The level of hygiene by modern standards was abysmal to non-existent. The presence of an ambulance was so common it passed almost unnoticed. Scarlet Fever, Diptheria, Measles and similar diseases, which in those days were killers, were a direct result of the prevailing insanitary conditions.

In spite of these adverse living conditions, and in retrospect, having grown up with them, we were unaware that we were so badly off. The Blocks children were tough, resilient and happy. Petty transgressions such as orchard raiding and the occasional foray into Annie Doyles' scrapyard were common but window and street lamp glass breaking were seldom if ever, deliberate and were more often the result of a miskick or an accidental push. Wickedness or disrespect for one's elders was conspicuous by its absence. I have no doubt that this was due entirely to the control over, and the example set, by our parents.

In such a closely-knit community, very little passed unnoticed, or unpunished. One whisper of a misdemeanour and the price had to be paid, sometimes two-fold. One by the person or persons sinned against, and two, by your own father when he became aware of it. Given such circumstances, moral standards were at a fairly high level and became habit.

Let is not be assumed from the last paragraph that we were paragons of virtue. Mischievous and sometimes borderline cases there were in plenty, for which dues were paid, but wickedness was so much the exception as to be almost a rarity.

There were three lobbies to each block. A "lobby" comprised four levels, access to which was by stone steps with iron balustrades or bannisters as we called them. On each level two doors faced each other across a landing. Behind these doors were two dwellings. The roof topping the eight houses was flat, with a 4-foot wall surrounding the whole. A dividing wall separated each lobby from the next.

This flat roof, or "Top house" as it was called, was intended for the drying of clothes. Also on the top house was an open-topped, cast iron tank. This was designed to carry 1,000 gallons of water to be used in case of fire. Inevitably the top houses became play areas, some of the more daring boys and more than one girl, walking around the 12-inch wide coping stone with a drop of 60 feet on the wrong side. Fortunately there were no mishaps in my life time. Testimony to the sure-footedness of the blocks boys and girls.

The water tanks, just as inevitably, became receptacles for all manner of rubbish, mainly discarded straw and flock mattresses.

One ground floor set of rooms in each block was designated as a communal wash house for that block. Many times have I stood in this steam-filled room with its huge boiler into which our mothers would plunge the family wash. The clothes would be "boiled", then at the appropriate moment, transferred to a tub. Here they would be swirled around violently with a three-legged stool-like contrivance. A centre pole about 3 feet long, having a cross rod handle inches from the top, was used to twist the three legs. This in turn rotated the clothes much as a modern machine might do.

A flagstone shelf, waist high, ran the length of the wall opposite the door. All the rubbing and scrubbing took place on these stones.

Three or four 'mangles' (hand propelled wooden rollers between which the sodden clothing would be squeezed almost dry), were strategically placed in the room. Sometimes a luckless boy would be roped in to turn the mangle wheel. This was an unpopular chore because of the football time lost.

One virtue which was there in abundance was a sense of humour. Even now, when recalling people and incidents, the mere mention of a name to an ex-blockite, will bring an instant roar of laughter. Among these characters was "Big Mary", otherwise known as the "Birkenhead News", or, "The Voice of them all". Mary was childless and so had plenty of time to observe. I well remember overhearing a remark she made concerning a young couple about to be married. It stayed with me although it was years before I understood the meaning of the remark which was — "Forced fruit will never keep." The inference being that the couple were obliged to marry therefore no good could come of it. Gossip, as her nick name suggests, was this lady's stock in trade. — Other names suggest good and bad, happy and sad times, but any old family name still evokes waves of nostalgia and affection for times past.

Our games were wide and varied and of necessity of our own making. The only indoor pastimes were board games such as Ludo and Snakes and Ladders. Cards and dominoes were common and cheap. Family sing-songs were also popular and a gramophone, wind-up type of course, was a treasure.

To a child, may be more so of our era, and most certainly to the children of "The Blocks", a rubber ball, or a cheap doll, or a box on wheels, not forgetting a mouth organ, was all that was needed for happiness. However, there were certain days which were special. Bonfire night was the culmination of dozens of special nights and days. Days and evenings were legitimately spent collecting wood from the plantation and rhododendron gardens, "The Rods" as we called them, and there were bonuses such as discarded straw mattresses which could be found in the disused 1000-gallon cast iron tanks on the "top houses", or roofs of the blocks. To carry such a mattress down four flights of stairs was a physical impossibility even to the strongest among us. The answer was patently obvious — to heave it over the 4-foot wall surrounding the top house.

This exercise was one of the highlights of our build-up to bonfire night. A straw mattress, weighted-down with months of soaked-up rain, hurtling down sixty feet, accompanied by screams of "look out below," to land with a sickening thud on the flagged block beneath, was a thrill that had to be experienced to be believed. Many sprint records, not to be found in the record books, were broken by unsuspecting persons, young and old, emerging from a lobby to the warning scream from above, to observe this huge rain-sodden mattress hurtling down from on high.

The illegitimate booty was the result of raids on other area bonfires. On these occasions the "Sentry" may be too scared to report his laxity to his street group, or a running battle would ensue until we arrived at our own fire site with our prize.

In retrospect, I believe that the preliminaries were much more exciting than the finale.

Corner shops played a vital part in Blocks life. Their owners names are part of Blocks history, from Ma Mutch, Liza Goldstone, Ellen Purcell, etc. Each shop merits a chapter unto itself but the very names suffice to recall an incident or incidents relative to that particular person or shop. Family names also have this effect. Just a few which come to mind are Charles McVey, Alderman and Mayor Birkenhead, (opened Arrowe Park Golf Club 1931), the Standings, Athertons, Stanleys, Leathleys (we called them Lakeleys), Lawtons, Thoms and numerous Davies's . . . I could go on and on recalling the names from my childhood, all with happy memories and never to be forgotten.

A sign of the times were the visits of half a dozen Lancashire miners who would walk up each block in line astern singing in harmony. When they had sung a song or two the leader would call out in a voice loud enough to carry up to four storeys, "If you can spare a copper without depriving yourself or your little **childer,** (not a mis-spelling) may God bless you."

Street traders also had their distinctive cries. Apart from our own "Pegs" Loudon, we had fish wives who, having pushed their handcarts from Hoylake would regale us with "Hoylake Fluke". I am told that they would sell herrings "5 for 1½-pence. — 40 for 1 shilling."

There were of course money lenders, one a long-bearded, black-coated, Mr. Sachs.

Another regular was our rag and bone man. A favourite game was to call after him — "Who plucked the duck?" His answer to this was always "Go and pluck your mother's duck." To this day I do not comprehend the meaning of the question or the answer.

Then we had the forerunner to the Ice Cream Brick. This gent would sell his product with the cry — "Hokey Pokey penny a lump, that's the stuff to make you jump." Later on when hygiene became tighter we had the box on wheels, Eldorado's "Stop me and buy one."

Salt also could be bought from a cart, 1 penny for a block, about as large as a house brick. A jug was always taken to the milk float to be filled from a churn.

A welcome addition to our lobby was the introduction by a Mr and Mrs Drysdale of the Emmanuels. These blue bonnetted, blue coated ladies held their religious meetings up our lobby and were, I believe, the original group now grown into the great organisation based in Palm Grove/Park Road South, sending missionaries all around the world.

Out of doors, football was our main preoccupation, games starting after our mid-day meal, being postponed when we had to dash back to school, to be resumed after tea and to continue until sunset.

With few exceptions our football was played on "The Oller". I imagine that this word was a derivation of "The Hollow" and years before could have been a defile, valley, or pit which as time passed had been filled in and then topped over with hard core and ashes. The end result was an area of land roughly the size of a football pitch, bounded on the Blocks side by Stewart Street and on the opposite side by Tyrer Street. The ends were at Stanley Road and Ilchester Road.

Roughly about two thirds up from Stanley Road were swings and shadles, (now known as "See-Saws".) The area up from Stanley Road was, by common consent, designated for football, and nowhere on earth was a football pitch used as was this cinder patch. I claim also, that this pitch produced more class football players and more importantly, sportsmen, than any other.

Among my contemporaries alone I could select a couple of dozen boys worthy to wear a Town, County — or even an odd one or two, England schoolboy shirt. Those of my year who were chosen were Sammy Loudon, Jack Lawton, Baden Garton and myself. Others, just as worthy, but unfortunately overlooked in our year, were such good ball players as

Cube Phillips, Billy Carrington, Hodge Stanley, Miffy Smith, the Standings, the Athertons, etc., etc.

Among the names of boys eligible in the years immediately before and after my time, were — The Myers brothers, Benny Poole, Fred Chamberlain, Joe and Tom Smith, Norman Fogg, the Standings, Walter Stanley, all the Loudon brothers, Billy Fogg, Norman Sutton, Pudding Johnson, Joe Wilson, Cecil and Frank Hayden, the Higgins brothers, Jerry Chamberlain, Teddy Sherlock, Ralph Beacall, Fred Creighton, Bill McLoughlan, Chilla Lawton, Dowster Kirby, . . . this list is endless, my memory fallible.

Most of these players graduated to top amateur and professional sides. Billy Fogg went to Huddersfield Town, Tom Malone to Rangers and Clydebank, Cecil Haydon to New Brighton, Doncaster and Derby County, and there were many unnamed who did likewise.

One remarkable fact concerning these players whose football apprenticeship was served on the "Oller" was that only at the Christmas period, when one boy's parents were "flush" and splashed out would a new football or as we called it a "Bladder" appear. This luxury would last about three weeks before the ashes surface wore through the leather case and we would be back to our usual "tanner" rubber ball. This we would acquire by pooling our weekend half pennies together. Maybe juggling this small ball laid the foundation for the undoubted footballing skills of most Blocks boys.

One fact which must be recorded is that 90% of these boys attended St. James School. This was situated where the library in Laird Street now stands. It was a small school with a tremendous success rate in the football world. Incidentally, I was not one of the 90%. My schools were Our Lady's in Price Street and St. Hugh's in Park Road South. The latter school, although 'young' by comparison with St. James, was beginning to emulate its rival on the soccer scene and games between us were always very keen and just as cleanly fought. In all modesty I must say that in my three years at St. Hugh's, we won both Junior and Senior Schools championships each year.

The girls played "Rounders" and the traditional girls' games such as 'Top and Whip', 'Ring O' Roses' and 'Hop Scotch' etc. "Relievo" was a mixed gender game, as were many more original games devised by the participants themselves.

One game which comes to mind was called appropriately "Throw your luggage out." This, by its very nature, was more of an initiation, the reason being that the principal participant was new to the area, or ignorant of the rules.

The "initiate" would be invited to be the "Station Master" to our human train. The honour would be too good to turn down. Whereupon he would be placed on his "station" whilst the "train" chugged off around the block. Once out of sight all manner of rubbish would be hurriedly collected and the return journey would commence, hands discreetly hidden behind one's back. On arrival at the "Station" the "Master", as directed, would call out — "Throw your luggage out." The whole "Train" would immediately oblige and the poor "initiate" would be smothered in a shower of indescribable "luggage".

Ball games would be played Winter and Summer and well into the late evening. The alternatives would be such as singing to a mouth organ. One could be bought for 6d or a shilling. Billy "Cobbler" Jackson, among others, was an expert on this instrument. "Sing Songs" were another alternative, and names which spring to mind in this connection are Ruby Williams and the Lazenby Brothers. Kitty Steen's accordion was also a much used instrument.

Games played on the top house, as the flat roofs were called, were frowned upon by our elders. Nevertheless there were games played which necessitated a chase up a lobby, four flights of stone steps, across the top house, down the next lobby, up the next, over the dividing wall and down the last lobby. Such games bred stamina and agility. Blocks children lacked neither.

BLOCKITE GOLF!

When a boy reached 11 or 12 years of age the lure of the golf course would prove irresistible and boys would be drawn as 'steel to a magnet'. A good caddy was not simply a bag-carrier-cum-ball-finder. He was a "tradesman" in that he had to be fluent in every aspect of the game. Golf has a language all of its own. Ethics also are vitally important. The terrain peculiar to each hole. The distance one can expect, given prevailing conditions and the players capabilities, determined the club to be recommended by the caddy. Last, but by no means least, he has to be an amateur psychologist. He must learn to know his man's moods and idiosyncrasies; encourage, but not patronise.

The wise boy would learn these facts and over the years build up a store of knowledge which is exemplified by the fact that today's professionals consider it very worthwhile to have "Travelling Caddies". If one watches closely the major tournaments one will see the leading golfers' caddies working alongside the same masters all over the world.

So it was at the West Cheshire and adjoining courses where the Blocks boys learned their trade. We had two or three brothers of one family, such as the Swanicks and Griffiths and even father and four sons, "Cobbler" Jackson and his sons, all of whom were in great demand. Incidentally, old "Cobbler" Jackson, originally of Hoylake, was a relative of the world famous Glenda Jackson.

When not caddying, the boys would be out on the course, shuffling through the "rough" searching for balls. There were a number of regular "Finders" — "Sparrow" Chamberlain, the Swannicks, Jack Phillips, "Lump" Fowler, "Dowster" Kirby, etc. etc. All these men were adept at ball finding, and I am sure they would admit now that many balls were 'found' before they were lost!

Many balls had what were known then as "dokers", that is scars or cuts on them. These men were expert at cleaning their finds up; filling in the "dokers", and then repainting. They were then sold as "repaints" and quite often kept the wolf from the door in this manner in hard times.

The West Cheshire Course was situated around what was the Wallasey Pool, (now Bidston Dock). The Pool was simply an irregularly shaped, grassy banked, stretch of water. On one side ran the Wrexham/Wallasey railway line, and on the other side and up to the road bridge, the golf course. The course followed the line of the pool and then took a right turn following the road past what is now the incinerator. It then went up to what is now the Co-op Coal depot, but which then was the railway engines sheds. It then took a right turn again, following what were the railway shed lines, up to what is now the motorway. It was a nice, undulating and interesting course and bred many fine golfers.

During the war the course was used as a decoy plot. Barrels of oil and tar were placed around and set alight to deceive the enemy into dropping their bombs harmlessly onto the open ground. In this they succeeded, but inevitably the club ended up with many more and larger bunkers than was originally planned.

The story of the West Cheshire Golf Club is now history, and maybe the club, its illustrious artisans section and individuals, could provide enough material for an interesting local history book.

Caddying was not only a pleasure, albeit a tiring one, it was also a source of income to a family. From 9 a.m. or so, on Saturday and Sunday, we would walk across to the course via the Railway Sheds.

The clubhouse itself was on one side of a dirt road which, starting at the first tee and going under the Wrexham/Wallasey Railway line bridge, would stretch for three or four hundred yards up hill to Breck Road, Poulton.

The Professionals Shop and Caddies Shed were on the opposite side of this sunken, dirt road. They were connected by a wooden bridge which lay alongside the railway bridge, both crossing the sunken dirt road at this point.

The Caddies' Shed was just that, an open-ended wooden structure, roofed with corrugated iron and having a dirt floor. Nothing here to encourage the lazy to lounge about.

The procedure was, that the "Toff", for that is what we called the club member, would cross the bridge to the Pro's shop, in our case Ern. Smith, whose assistant, later to become famous, was Norman Sutton. Ern. or Norman would open up a trap door about 5' up the shed wall, and unless the "Toff" had expressed a preference for a particular caddy, the next man or boy on the list would be handed the bag of clubs and join his man on the first tee.

Needless to say as a weekend only caddy, my name would be way-down the list. Very often one could be present all day without success. In this case the day would be spent practising chipping and putting in the field. Meanwhile a sharp lookout was kept for a "Toff" crossing the bridge. There would then be a mad scramble to see who he was and who would get his bag.

If successful, and one got a bag, the fee was one shilling and threepence, or 6 to 7 pence in our money today. If your man was generous, you might get one shilling and six pence or even two shillings. (10-pence today).

These figures look ridiculous by today's standards, but in those days if I took home one shilling and sixpence, my mother would add another shilling which would cover the cost of a piece of brisket from Halliwells, the butcher in Laird Street. This would be enough to provide a Sunday joint for mother, father and five children.

A plus factor also was that one had walked four or five miles in the fresh air carrying a weighty bag of clubs. Quite a feat for a 11/12 year old, but a very rewarding chore from any point of view.

Most "Blocks" caddies were far better golfers than the gentlemen for whom they carried. Most of them were able to judge shots and distances to the yard. In later years I learned of "Blocks" caddies who had travelled world-wide with golfers of international fame. One among many coming to mind was "Chloey" Atherton, regular caddie to Christie O'Connor Senior. These men travelled the world at their patrons' expense, but unfortunately the majority failed to take advantage of the monetary rewards, which were often frittered away.

Thankfully there were those who turned the knowledge and skills gained by their initial grounding to very good effect.

Tales have been told of the experiences of some of these caddies on their travels, most of them unprintable. However, one tale told to me by Jack Calveley, an old stager, concerns Kirk Douglas, the famous film star. It appears that Jack was carrying for Kirk Douglas, a very wealthy man, at Hoylake. They had finished the round and the rich Mr Douglas enquired of the professional, the caddie's fee. On being told that £1 was the usual, Jack was elated to hear Mr Douglas say, "What! £1! Jack has been worth much more than that to me today." Calveley had visions of £10-£20 notes. With these American millionaires, who knows, the sky could be the limit. As these lovely thoughts were going through his mind, Kirk Douglas, his dimpled smile well in evidence, thrust a pound note — plus two half crowns, into his hand.

In fairness to our American friends, it must be said, that in the main, they are generous to a fault.

West Cheshire Artisans

Most golf clubs had what is known as the "Artisans" section. The word "artisan" means, of course, "mechanic" — "workman" or "handicraftman". The choice of word was, I suppose, quite deliberate, and in those class-conscious days it would be quite acceptable to differentiate between the "gentleman" club member, who paid his full fee, and the "artisan" or "tradesman" who paid a minimal fee and rendered services around the course for the privilege of being a member with certain restrictions. So it was at our local club, "West Cheshire."

Up to the club's sad demise, West Cheshire Artisans were probably the most successful in the north, if not in the country.

The Sutton brothers, Bill the elder of the two, and Norman, triumphed so often, it was almost expected of them to do so. Their remarkable records stand as follows:—

Bill Sutton   English Amateur Champion 1929, 1936
                    Runner up . .   1935, 1938, 1946
                    Cheshire Amateur Champion 1921, 1926, 1927.

Norman Sutton Cheshire Champion 1928.
                    Turned Professional 1929 — Club Leigh, Lancs G.C.
                    Moved to Exeter G.C.
                    Won British Senior P.G.A. Championship 1958.

The Senior World professional golf championship is decided by a match between the American senior champion and the British champion. As a result of his success in 1958, Norman Sutton was matched against Gene Sarazen and after a thrilling match triumphed to become World Champion.

Many times we looked down from four storeys high on to a sea of bobbing heads and listened to the acclamation given to one or other of the Sutton boys as they were carried shoulder high up and down each block.

It is difficult to say which of the brothers achieved the greatest success, in his day. Bill, for sheer consistency over a long and brilliant amateur career, or Norman, by his single, wonderful triumph as World Professional Golfers Association Champion. The choice is yours. We were, and are, equally proud of both.

Whilst the Suttons were the most illustrious of our golfing fraternity, there were many more successes to be attributed to this remarkable Artisans Section. "Algo" Burton won the Artisans' championship in 1924. On May 1st 1938, my own brother-in-law, Teddy Sherlock, achieved the almost impossible, a clean sweep in the "News of the World Northern Artisans' Championship."

The tournament was over two days — the events —

Best nett score on day one   — winner — E. Sherlock.
Best scratch score on day two   — winner — E. Sherlock.
Best aggregate score on both days — winner — E. Sherlock.
Team event won by Ralph Beacall, Jim Loudon and E. Sherlock.

Ted Sherlock's prize list read like a Jewellers/Sports Outfitters catalogue. — "News of the World" Trophy plus solid silver replica; gold pocket watch; gold wrist watch; silver teapot; two leather golf bags plus six golf balls. A photograph taken of him carrying his trophies reminded me of a modern day superstore prizewinner carrying away as much as he could gather in an allotted time. — Teddy was a great golfer and a great friend as well as a brother-in-law.

"Poll's Jags."

Apart from being the mother of the two famous Sutton brothers, Poll had two other very good artisan golfer sons, John and Ernest. She was also famous locally in her own right.

Highly paid executives are employed by famous companies to conjure up eye-catching names for their products, world-famous names such as "Hoover" being synonymous with cleaners; "Ever Ready" with batteries, etc. Poll Sutton's name was synonymous with "Jags". Most of the youths, most certainly caddies, would gather in Poll's to partake of her "Jags." What were they? Simply pie and peas — plus of course golf talk. Who scored what, when and where; prospects for jobs at local courses. In fact anything connected, however remotely, with golf, was discussed and digested along with "Poll's Jags".

The "Blocks" but not the "Blocks"

We always considered Stanley Court and Stanley Road to be of the Blocks but not in them. Here again we had families and individuals who contributed greatly to the scene of that era. The Loudon family were prominent in this respect and Percy ("Pegs") was probably the best known of all the seven brothers.

Mrs Loudon owned a newsagents/sweet shop in Stanley Road opposite to the Tapestry Works, the history of which is referred to on page 34. "Pegs" was the paper delivery boy, although the term "delivery boy" in this instance was a complete misnomer. "Pegs" would simply stand in the middle of a block every evening and Sunday morning, and in a voice which was quite distinctive and familiar to every man, woman and child in the Blocks would call out, "Echo, Express", or on Sundays, "Umpire", "News of the World." This call would bring the customers scurrying down the lobby stairs clutching their pennies to relieve "Pegs" of a newspaper. After two or three positional changes, the huge armful of papers would have disappeared up the lobbies and Percy would scarcely have moved above a few yards. I am not aware of the number of papers Percy disposed of in this manner but I do know that he held the monopoly in the Blocks for many years, in fact until Jones's took a cabin opposite to St. James Church.

Newspapers were the only source of information until the advent of Radio, which did not develop until years later as a news medium. Even then the average family could ill-afford to buy this new contraption, so newspapers were assured of their position in this field for years to come.

"Pegs" was one of seven sporting brothers, being a very good forward, playing for Birkenhead Nomads. All the brothers were golfers and footballers, some playing both games to a high standard. Sam was my friend and colleague with Birkenhead Schoolboys, later playing, as did his brothers for leading amateur clubs.

Our Blocks "Chippy" was situated in Stanley Road. Mrs Chamberlain's "pennorth" was equivalent in quantity to a present-day 30 or 35 pence bag. The wrapping could be a day-old "Echo", a bonus if you had not been able to afford the penny for that edition.

Mrs "Packer" Francis took over this vital cog in the Blocks machinery on Mrs Chamberlain's retirement.

Below the Chamberlain's in Stanley Road was Davies' Veg Shop, home of Ethel Davies, midwife, who assisted so many newcomers into the world, including yours truly. Tom Davies, another West Cheshire Artisan, was a son who carried on, in later years, a similar business opposite to Bidston Church. Other families in Stanley Road which spring to mind are the Myers (all the boys in this family were first-class amateur footballers and equally proficient at golf, the Creightons, the McLoughlins, the Edwards, the McColgans (the eldest boy, Eddie, was tragically drowned off Leasowe), the Riches, etc.

Stanley Court, which bisected the main Blocks from the Stanley Road/Stewart Street triangle complex, also housed families which were synonomous with the area — Calveleys, Phillips, Palmers, Swannicks, Moffats, Bill Pooles, Williams, Cash's, etc.

Up Stewart Street, and virtually next door to the "Blood Tub" was the locally famous "Mary Lizzies", a home-made brawn shop. Lizzie Garton, the daughter of Mrs Davies of Stanley Road Veg Shop, produced the most delicious brawn, which, with the advantage of present day marketing techniques, would have made her fortune. Her son, Baden, was another member of the same Birkenhead Schoolboys team of my year. He and his elder brother later became Artisan golfers.

A door or so away was Aggie Humphrey's Pop Shop. "Pop" in this context was the soft drink, not a pawn shop. Many evenings were spent by the local youths chatting and discussing life in general, mainly sport, over a penny bottle of pop, sasparilla or dandelion and burdock, just as our elders did over their beers a few doors away. The family names I can recall in this section were the Johnsons, McDonnells, Toppings, Murphys, and Wilsons whose front door was under Wilkinson's archway.

Wilkinsons' Bakery and shop was on the corner of Stewart Street and Stanley Court and must have been one of, if not the oldest, established businesses in the area. Never, since leaving the Blocks at sixteen years of age, have I tasted bread the equal of that baked by Wilkinson's Master Baker and Ken Smale, his assistant. Crisp and crusty tin loaves, oven bottoms or cottage loaves, all were to be savoured and remembered, especially when confronted by today's apology for bread.

Lilian Wilkinson and her sister, Mrs Smale, staffed the shop, entry into which was an experience in itself. The smell of freshly baked bread mingled with the aroma of heady spices, assailed the nostrils. Surrounding the shop on all but the door side, was a 3-foot wide counter, scrubbed clean. Against the counter on the customers' side were wooden bins about 4-foot square with flap lids. These bins contained a variety of cereals and grades of flour.

Deliveries were made by Wilf Leach, whose mother was a Wilkinson. In later years he married Lil Dean, sister of the immortal Dixie. Wilf took the bread around in a horse-drawn, closed van, later to be replaced by a motor van.

Ken Smale has recounted to me a story of those early horse-drawn days when it had been his job to see the horse safely stabled after deliveries. The stable was situated on that plot of land now bordered by Stanley Road, Townsend Street and Gautby Road. The horse, a large grey, was normally docile and obedient. On this occasion he decided that, contrary to orders from Ken, he was not going to slow down on the approach to the stable area, the gateway of which was headed by a thick wooden lintel. The result was that Ken was not able to duck in time and was swept off the horse's back to land ignominiously in the usual stable area droppings.

On the opposite side of Gautby Road and taking in the flats and the first few houses now in Gautby Road and Patricia Avenue, was another clutch of stables, one of which housed Herbert Wilkinson, the milkman's horse and trap. Bert Wilkinson, another member of this respected business family, at a later date garaged his ancient Ford coal lorry directly opposite Ken's stables and next door to Annie Doyles' yard.

The whole of the area, with the exception of these stables on the railway side of Gautby Road, was green field up to Bidston Station and School Lane and beyond to Leasowe, all owned by Lord Vyner.

My brother, Joe, was driver of Bert's ancient Ford wagon and I earned a few coppers cleaning it on Sundays. On one occasion I succeeded in starting the motor, much to my amazement. Stopping it was another matter. I tried everything within my limited knowledge which, at 11 years of age, was almost zero. Panic stricken, I eventually decided to risk life and limb by extracting the plugs one by one, a very painful process, until the engine stopped.

Although the "Blocks" were comprised of the two main religious factions, Catholic and Protestant, (alphabetical order), any strong feeling would only manifest itself on the two main event days of the year, 17th March, St. Patrick's day, and 12th July, Orangeman's day. The latter was the more boisterous because of the Fife and Drums band. This group was led by a Mr Probyn of Tollemache Road. This gentleman would lead the band up one block and down the next until they had walked via every block, from St. James' Church to the "Oller."

These marches were never without incident. It was not unknown for the contents of a chamber pot to be liberally spread over the band having started its journey three or four storeys up.

The same Mr Probyn who led the Orange band with his twirling staff also officiated as Fireman at the "Laides" or Palladium, our nearest picture house in Price Street, near Duke Street.

Admission to the Saturday morning Children's show was 1½ pence, (old money). During these shows, pandemonium reigned. The pictures then were of course silent and invariably cowboys and indians.

Girls as well as boys would be standing on the seats yelling encouragement or derision, whichever was appropriate to the scene.

When Mr Probyn had decided that his accepted decibel limit had been exceeded, he would reach the offender with his 12 or 15-foot thin, bamboo pole. A sharp tap on the top of the head would bring that particular child back from the prairie to the seat in the "Laides", ardour cooled albeit temporarily.

The "Laides" is a milestone in my life in that it was there that I sat through my first "Talkie."

THE BLOOD TUB

The hub of the men's world was the "Blood Tub", never ever referred to by its official name of "The New Dock Hotel". Less favoured was "Murphy's", so called after the boss at that time, but officially "The Graving Dock Hotel."

In these establishments, world-shattering decisions were made over a pint of "Higsons" ale in the Blood Tub, or "Yates" ale in Murphy's.

As youngsters, we would hang around the Blood Tub at "chucking out" time, when our education would be considerably extended to cover subjects not to be found in school text books.

Occasionally the discussions would turn to arguments and, on occasion, fisticuffs. An invaluable lesson to be learned when this stage was reached was the meaning of "fair play". Never did I witness any questionable act during such altercations. It was an unwritten law that nobody interfered with the participants. The usual cry as soon as a clash became inevitable was, "Give them room." After honour had been satisfied, things would return to normal and probably at the next opening time the contestants would be sharing a pint.

The original Blood Tub of the '20s, tales about which are legion, stood at the corner of Stanley Road and Stewart Street. Mine host in those days was Jack Allen. Amongst prominent customers' names of that period were, Ike Grey, "Swilly" Stanley, his brother, Bob; Frank, "Buddy" and "Beef" Standing, Jackie Mack, the Swannicks, Calvelies & Pooles, "Scouse" Davies' family, Joe (Wass) Davies, etc, etc. "All good pals and jolly good company!"

It was inevitable that, among hard men and equally hard drinkers, differences of opinion would arise, sometimes mild, but often acrimonious. The latter type inevitably led to what was colloquially known as a "punch up". However, even when this stage was reached, things were never allowed to develop into a sordid "brawl". Drunk or sober, rules of fair play were strictly adhered to at all times.

The prelude to one particular "punch up" took place in the old "Blood Tub", one summer's evening.

The protagonists in this particular drama were two shipmates of the old "Blue Funnel Line", or "China boats." A ship's crew can number literally dozens of men, according to tonnage. In this instance, these two men were not just shipmates, they shared the same boiler room, shoulder to shoulder.

Jackie Mack was no shrinking violet, nor was he a braggart. He was simply known as a tough man with whom one did not take liberties. Tom Silverwood was a more reserved type but equally one would hesitate to take liberties with this very inoffensive giant. He topped 6 foot, while Mack was probably just under; pound for pound they would be very much the same — about 14 stones.

Ships in those days were coal fired, every pound having to be shovelled into the furnaces by men like Mack and Sylvester, and this for thousands of miles — to Australia; China; India, etc., day in and day out. I have seen the hands of these men at close quarters, Jackie Mack's particularly, because he eventually became my brother-in-law. Their hands were iron hard and the palms were permanently black. They had huge segs or callouses and crevices, thick with irremovable coal dust, which, starting between the fingers at the palm, went through to the back of the knuckles.

What, you might ask, could provoke two intimate friends, who had shared thousands of miles of toil, under the most appalling conditions, and who had joined each other at a bar to enjoy a drink, to suddenly engage in such an argument that it resulted in a fight. The answer was, simply, a spilled drink.

I have never been able to ascertain which of them knocked over the other's drink. Suffice it to say that the "Blood Tub" doors opened and out stepped the two giants, followed by the full house, including the barmen, and the manager, Jack Allen.

The chosen venue was on the corner opposite — a cinder patch outside Davies's garden on the site of what is now the end of Townsend Street and Stanley Road.

As was usual, they stripped to the waist, and, as was also usual, nobody interfered, except of course with verbal encouragement or advice.

After fifteen minutes, or so, when both were exhausted, partly from their exertions, but mainly through drink, the exposed upper halves of their bodies were lacerated by contact with the cinders, and by mutual consent an end was called.

The unsatisfactory ending satisfied neither of the parties, so a return fight was arranged on the spot. This was not for the next week, when wounds and lacerations may have been expected to heal, but for the very next morning — Sunday.

As mentioned earlier, fights in those days, and in that area, were never tawdry brawls with weapons other than fists being used. They were fought, the combatants not even aware of it, almost to the Marquis of Queensbury' rules. In this instance, my father, an ex-professional boxer himself, was automatically elected to arrange and referee the contest. He promptly declared that the fight would resume at 8.30 a.m. the next morning and the venue would be a natural grassy ampitheatre on the then, West Cheshire Golf Course. He had chosen well. The "ring" was on a sunken fairway surrounded by hillocks upon which it seemed that hundreds of spectators vied with each other for the best vantage points to witness this battle of two modern "gladiators."

Both men, bare fisted and again stripped to the waist, listened to Dad's orders which were succinct. "Nothing below the belt. When one has had enough, raise your hand and step back."

The bout lasted about twenty minutes before Tom Silverwood, bloody but unbowed, raised a weary and broken fist in surrender. They fell into each other's arms in a gesture of mutual respect, hobbled off to the adjacent Wallasey Pool, now Bidston dock, and dived in. Afterwards they walked arm in arm up to the "Blood Tub", and returned to their ship some days later. They remained bosom pals until death.

Chapter 3
SCHOOL DAYS TO DANCE BAND DAYS

IMPRESSIONS AND INFLUENCES

First impressions, especially in formative years, are like small foundation stones in the house of life. Once laid, for good or evil, they are there to stay. Life thereafter is coloured by this or that word or gesture, spoken or made, during these early years.

Apart from the obvious experiences and examples from family life, memories from as early as 'commencing schooling' are still fresh in my mind. I recall setting out on my short life's first adventure; finding my own way to school.

I suspect that my sisters, quite rightly, had grown tired of the chore of escorting me to school each day to deposit me at the Infants' department of Our Lady's. It must have been decided by my parents that I should have a 'dummy run' because I was aware that a hundred yards or so behind me on a particular day, was one or other of my sisters — Ann, Lou or May. This exercise must have been considered a success because the very next day I was shocked to learn that from henceforth I was to be alone.

The distance from 'G' Block, Dock Cottages, must have been less than one mile from Our Lady's School. To me, a six year old, it seemed like a journey into the unknown.

The first steps were across and up Ilchester Road, around Tom Malone's and Bill Ashley's coal yard, across a waste patch of land and into Corporation Road. At the corner of Corporation Road and Laird Street, was McCormicks' General Store. If one chose to stay on that, the right hand side, there were, and still are, the same line of houses which culminated in the wall surrounding St. James' School, and up to Miriam Place.

Across Miriam Place you would be confronted by a still higher wall. This formidable barrier surrounded the Albert Industrial School. This wall's end was at Lincoln Street. From there, and forming a great triangle with Lansdowne Road, was a plot of land enclosed entirely in eight foot sheets of corrugated iron. The apex of this triangle ended at a point opposite the bottom of Milner Street. This corrugated iron corner was, tragically, to be the scene of the death of a famous Canadian film and stage star in later years — Bonar Colleano. For some inexplicable reason, he drove his car into the iron-sheeted corner instead of proceeding straight on up Corporation Road. Across the road and still on the right hand side, the old houses continued down to Patten Street. From that point and along Price Street, the Church and the School were in sight.

The walk down the left hand side was quite different. The first sighting after the coal yard would be allotment railings stretching to a point opposite to Miriam Place and ending simply in a dirt road or lane. Over the lane was the Industrial School playing field, extending to opposite the end of Lincoln Street and reaching down to the railway. More fenced fields followed and then the rear walls of defunct factories as far down as Patten Street.

Continuing on the left hand side one would come to a rough, grassy area. This was known as Gallaghers hill. The term "Hill", as with many other names of our time, was a complete misnomer, because from Price Street, the land fell away into a defile with a small pit, usually refuse filled.

So much for my first geographical impressions of this big world into which I was taking my first, tentative steps. Now what about people and personalities.

After parental influence one followed naturally under the influence of surrogate parents — school teachers. In this respect I was most fortunate throughout school life.

Again women, certainly in the earlier years, dominated the scene, the Misses Crowley, Mrs O'Brien, Miss Simms and Miss Harding, daughter of the head teacher. On reflection it was Miss Harding, the youngest member of the staff, who raised a small question in my young mind. The "Blocks" ladies, and my own mother, the only adult females I had encountered to that date, were, in the main, scrubbed clean and wholesome smelling. Somehow this lady, who came close to me to read my efforts or to talk to me, was different.

It took a little while before my childish mind found the answer. — Smell! A pleasant smell, but not more so than the soap smell I had been used to. Miss Harding's smell was, of course, make-up, powder, scent, etc., commodities not over indulged in around my place of birth.

From eleven to school leaving at fourteen-and-a-half, were the most impressionable years of early life. This period was spent in a school to which we graduated for the remainder of our education — St. Hugh's in Park Road South.

Just before the school's closure, in 1982, having opened in 1922, Mr M.N. Ryan, acting headmaster, honoured me by asking me to contribute a chapter to a book on the history of the school. I decided that my impressions of the school, as I had seen it on those first days, would be appropriate. So, "Reminiscences of an old boy" was published, as follows —

It was a daunting prospect to this eleven year old, to be told that I was soon to leave the almost 100% matriarchal atmosphere of Our Lady's School and be catapulted to St. Hugh's School, where rumour had it, the only soft, female influence was that of the lady cleaners on the school furniture. The Staff at St. Hugh's was 100% male. Not even a secretary to redress the balance.

In a short discourse on the merits of this comparatively new establishment to which we were destined to go, Mr Harding, our headmaster, assured us that the educational foundations laid by our worthy class mistresses, Mrs O'Brien, Miss Simms, Miss Harding, and the Sisters Crowley, would ensure that we were worthy of our new status. The fact that he added that we would be joining "Foreigners" from St. Werburgh's, St. Lawrence's and St. Joseph's was cold comfort indeed.

My first impression of my new school was of open-mouthed wonder. This was no conventional school building. It was a beautiful old mansion surrounded by immaculate lawns and magnificent shrubs, flowers and trees, all maintained by the boys themselves under the tutelage of a Mr Marmion.

I recall it took just two or three lessons with our first year masters to discover that our fears regarding the "Heavy hand of man" were groundless. Each master had his own individual approach to his job and all, without exception, proved to be efficient, firm, just and ever willing to listen. Without exception also, each possessed a sense of humour.

It is worth recording at this stage that I cannot recall one instance of resentment by a pupil for a beating by a master. In fact, the master who left my fingers tingling on more than one occasion for what he considered was my laziness in Algebra, was then, and was until he died, the man I admired the most. It was my pleasure and privilege to visit him very often in his retirement at his bungalow overlooking Flaybrick hill cemetary — the late Roger O'Donnell.

The whole school exuded 'Esprit de Corps'. Academically, on the sportsfield and most importantly, in being one of, what we all considered ourselves to be, a St. Hugh's boy and therefore untouchable.

This feeling of pride in our school was enhanced by what was to me, the most distinctive uniform in town. In fact, in my subsequent travels all over Great Britain, I have yet to see its equal. The blazer was all green with a yellow swan on the breast pocket. The cap was likewise green with the yellow swan on the front. The button on top of the cap was coloured according to that allotted to the house to which you belonged — Vincentian - Benedictine - Franciscan or Dominican.

I was fortunate enough to gain certain sporting honours, alas the only extra academic honour being a Royal Society of Arts pass in English. None gave me greater pleasure than gaining the right as a prefect, to change my yellow swans to silver, and the right, accorded to masters and prefects only, to use the front entrance and gates. Small things which meant a lot.

St. Hugh's produced many fine men, sporting and academic. My own fifth form also produced at least three Priests, Fathers Bob Fallon, Barry O'Brien and Arthur McGrath whose younger brother is also a priest. John Jones, before taking his final vows, changed his vocation, retiring a few years ago as Assistant Head of Rock Ferry St. Ann's. Another form pal, John Hynes, retired Head Master of St. Werburgh's.

If, as I hope, this wonderful spirit has continued over the years, I can imagine "Old boys" meeting 50 years hence and reminiscing as I do now with my contemporaries. I sincerely hope that they will part with the words — 'ST. HUGH'S — BEATAE MEMORIAE' (St. Hugh's of blessed memory).

Officially my school life ended at fourteen years, but I was 'encouraged to stay on by the Senior English Master, Mr Murphy' so that I could sit a Royal Society of Arts examination in English. I cannot remember where he took me to sit this examination. All I know is that I was quite alone in a room and that I justified his confidence in me.

The other teacher who encouraged me to stay on, but for a different reason, was Frank Butler. Frank had a friend in Liverpool Cotton Exchange who had promised him that he would see me in a few months time regarding an interview for a job.

Eventually the time came around and, dressed in best 'bib and tucker', I crossed on the ferry to Liverpool with my mother, carrying a letter of introduction to the gentleman on the Cotton Exchange.

The result of the interview was favourable and my mother I know, was proud that her son would soon be joining this prestigious body, the Liverpool Cotton Exchange. On the boat home, however, she sensed that I was not too happy and enquired the reason why. I told her that I could not envisage working in the atmosphere prevailing in the Exchange building.

Although this must have been a bitter disappointment to her, both from a financial angle and also the sense of pride in the job to be, she immediately acquiesced and I stayed on at school a little longer.

Shortly afterwards I became interested in my friend Eric Ekblom's tales about his job at Yelverton Dawbarns, the door makers, and within one month I was the first apprentice joiner to be employed by Yelverton Dawbarns, West Float, Birkenhead (on the Wallasey side, opposite to the Graving Dock).

"First impression!" Who knows how life in later years is affected by these two little words. In this instance, I was plunged from a cossetted school atmosphere, where I had been on the receiving end of a degree of adulation, due to my sporting activities, into a world where survival was strictly on merit and the ability to 'pull one's weight' was the criteria.

Whilst my first job in Dawbarns factory was as a boy assistant to a wood machinist, as mentioned above, in a short space of time I became the first apprentice joiner at Europe's biggest door factory.

The men who initiated me into this business were, without exception, a group of gentlemen. Each was a character unto himself. Each was kind and considerate and mindful of the fact that I was but a boy among men. All taught me dignity and self respect. Alas, they could not teach me their trade because, although my indentures described me as a "joiner", and these men were genuine joiners, doormaking consisted mainly of the use of a heavy rubber-headed mallet for eight hours a day. I did not learn joinery but I could boast of biceps and triceps worthy of a circus 'strong man'.

The Author (on the right) with the Carlton Collegians in 1938. Also in the picture John Williams (Drums), Bill Collins (Tenor Sax & Accordion), Sammy Barr (Vocalist), Roland West (Alto Sax) and Vernon Bissell (Piano & Accordion).

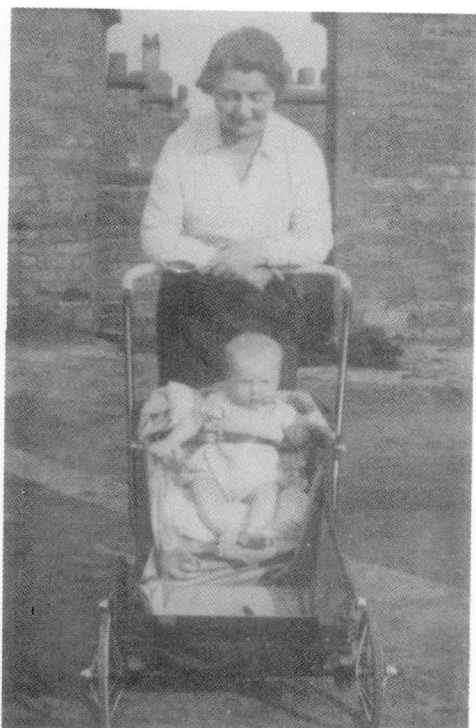

Mother Houldin & Grandaughter

Grandma Houldin

FRONT ELEVATION.

BACK ELEVATION.

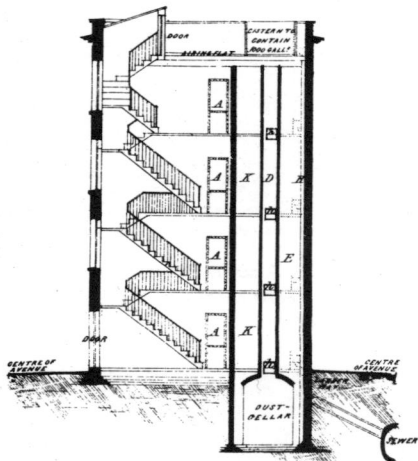

SECTION THROUGH STAIRCASE

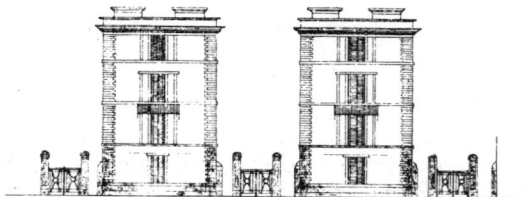

ENTRANCE TO ONE OF THE AVENUES.

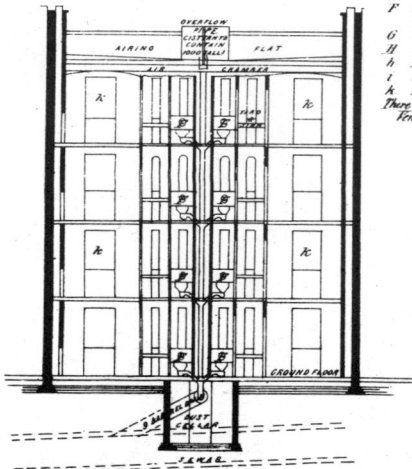

REFERENCE TO DETAILED PLAN & SECTIONS.

A. Entrance to Dwelling
B. Living Room
C. Bed Rooms
D. Dust Shaft common to the 8 Dwellings & leading to the Dust Cellar in the Basement
E. Vertical Shaft to contain the Soil Gas & Water Pipes, & of sufficient sectional area to admit a Workman
F. Water Closet with Trapped Pan. Wooden Seat turned up.   The Closet is so contrived that no person can use it without shutting himself in, & he cannot leave it without again shutting the door
G. Sink. The Water from which runs through the Trapped Pan into
H. The Soil pipe, into Drain, into Sewer
h. Hole with Iron Shutter into Dust Shaft.
i. Over Flow Pipe from Cistern for Flushing the Soil Pipe and Drains.
k. The Windows.
There will be Air Flues & Air Bricks with Iron Shutters to each Room in all the Dwellings for the purpose of Ventilation

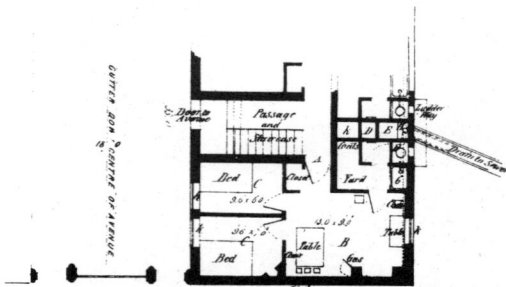

SECTION SHEWING THE ARRANGEMENT OF THE SINKS, WATERCLOSETS AND DRAINS.

PLAN

Plan published in The Liverpool Journal Newspaper 1845.

PLANS,
ELEVATIONS & SECTIONS
of
FIREPROOF DWELLINGS,
For the
WORKMEN OF THE BIRKENHEAD DOCK COMPANY
Now in Progress of Erection at
BIRKENHEAD.

Presented to the Subscribers of the
LIVERPOOL JOURNAL NEWSPAPER.
May 3rd 1845.

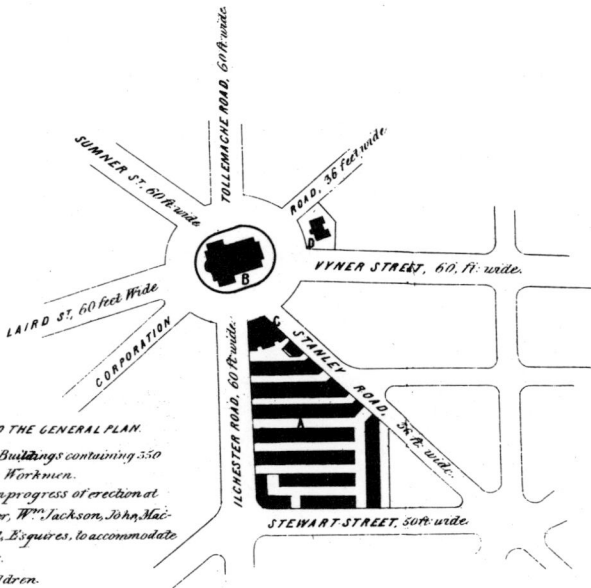

REFERENCE TO THE GENERAL PLAN.

A. Site of the Company's Buildings containing 550 dwellings for their Workmen.

B. Church endowed & in progress of erection at the cost of Wm Potter, Wm Jackson, John Macgregor & Wm Laird, Esquires, to accommodate 1000 adult persons.

C. Schools for 500 Children.

D. Parsonage House

a.a.a. Drains from Houses into

b.b.b. Sewers to Main Sewer in Street.

THE DIRECTORS OF THE BIRKENHEAD DOCK COMPANY finding that they must either provide accommodation for the numerous Workmen required for the construction of their Warehouses & Docks, or submit to great inconvenience, expense & delay in consequence of the want of it, have determined to erect a number of Dwellings for their Labourers and Mechanics. After calculating the cost & returns from various descriptions of Cottages submitted to them, they have decided to build to the accompanying Plans, designed by C. E. Lang, Esqr considering that by their adoption, the greatest amount of comfort will be afforded the occupiers, that can be combined with a fair return upon the Capital invested.

Each dwelling will have an unlimited supply of Water, a Gas light, & all rates & taxes will be paid by the Company, the Tenant paying in One fixed sum per week, all charges incident to the occupation of his Dwelling.

Birkenhead, 7th April, 1845.

MACGREGOR LAIRD
Secretary.

STANLEY Buildings

New Dock Hotel

Urinal

STEWART STREET

FRYER STREET

Block K

Block J

Block G

Block H

DOCK COTTAGES

Block F

Block E

Block D

Block C

Block B

Block A

STANLEY ROAD

B.M. 33·1

B.M. 33·8

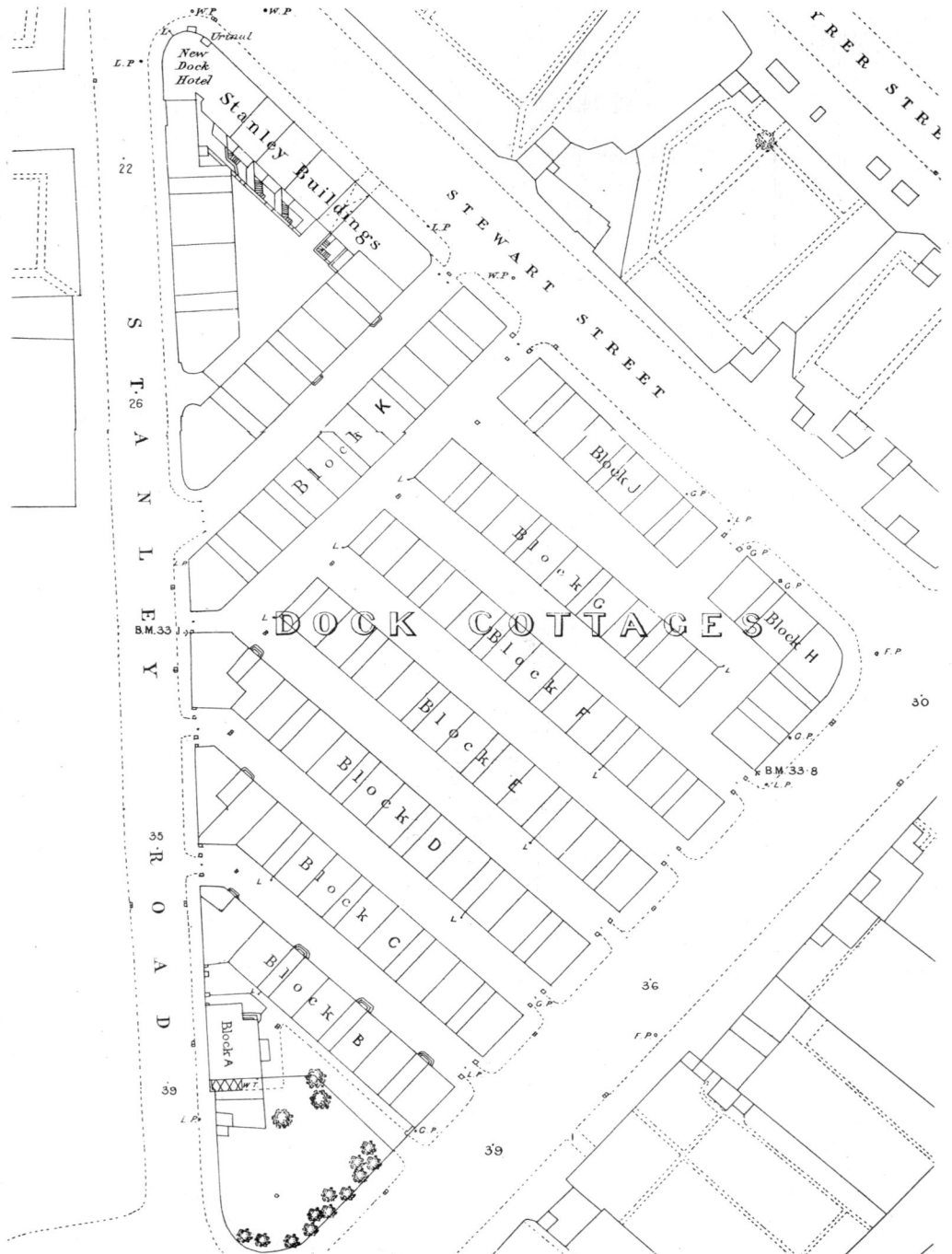

Detailed plan of Dock Cottages. From Ordnance Survey, 10ft. to the Mile Map of 1875. (Courtesy of The Ordnance Survey).

26

Blocks K & D viewed from the Lee Tapestry works where excavations for a 2nd Weaving Shed were taking place. (Williamson Art Gallery & Museum Collection).

Dock Cottages from Stanley Road in the early 1900's. Note large gate posts between blocks. (Local History Collection, Birkenhead Central Library).

Ariel view from the opposite direction to that shown overleaf, taken at the same time (Oct 1936). (Williamson Art Gallery & Museum Collection).

Two views of the new Dock Hotel (The Blood Tub).

St. James Church with the Dock Cottages in the background. The letter A is just distinguishable on the first block. Early 1900's.
(Local History Collection, Birkenhead Central Library.)

Passageway between Block D & E. *The* letter D can be clearly seen on the end of the block, the gate posts have now gone

"The Beginning of the End". Demolition of Block 'H' in progress. Block G where the Houldins lived can be seen in the right of the picture. (Local History Collection, Birkenhead Central Library).

34

The gentlemen, whose code of conduct I endeavoured to copy, were — Charles Redhead, George Wilcox, a member of one of Bidston, School Lane's, oldest families, Bob Kendrick, Joe Penny, Bill Webster, Jack Lucas, Ted Pugh, Harry Pearce, Hugh Meikle — one of the walking race Meikle brothers, the Nesbitt brothers, Bob and Arthur, plus their father. Last, but by no means least, was my dear friend, Owen Davies. Owen was probably the youngest of the men and was my closest friend and confidante. All the mysteries of life encountered by a boy, from puberty, through adolescence, youth to manhood, I was able to discuss with Owen. All would be explained in a tasteful and discreet manner by this gentlest of men.

Our joiners' boy, or 'sweeper-up', was Rob "Ginger" Griffiths. He it was who introduced me to the piano accordion and to the Conway Boxing Club. He was already, at that early age, proficient at both. He boxed successfully many times and then forsook the ring and Dawbarns to join a celebrated musical act, "The Seven Elliotts" with whom he travelled Europe.

"Ginger" was also responsible for my love of motor cycles. He approached me in a very conspiratorial manner one day, to suggest I go with him to the "Black Shed." This was a large warehouse painted black, empty save for lines of concrete supports running its length. In this shed one of the two Lambert brothers, joiners, kept a huge Harley Davidson motor bike.

It required our combined strength to hold this monster, and the idea was that I was supposed to try to ride this machine while Robby ran alongside supporting me. Needless to say, Mr Lambert was blissfully unaware that his machine was being used in this way.

In 1937 I acquired what was at that time the "Rolls Royce" of motor cycles, a 250 cc Sunbeam; price, brand new, on the instalment plan — £68 at 10/- per week.

Robby's accordian-playing planted a love for the instrument within me. The result was that I bought one and was introduced to a Bill Owens (whose band I subsequently joined), who undertook to teach me the rudiments of the instrument for 6d a lesson. Unfortunately I soon discovered that I had a natural aptitude for playing the instrument by ear. Consequently I became too lazy to learn music, neglecting the intricacies of bass and key board harmonies. This deception was aided, unwittingly, by the brilliant accordianists with whom I played. They provided the essential harmonies thereby covering up for my shortcomings, on my bass work, etc. My contribution was in the main on vocals, and on balance, this was probably considered an acceptable share.

Local exponents of the instruments who come to mind, were Bill Morris, Bill Collins, Tommy Lyndon, Rob Fawcett and Robby Griffiths, already mentioned.

Being a vocalist, my main preoccupation was with pianists. The number I worked with are too numerous to mention, but among the locals I can think of are, firstly the man who accompanied me on my first engagement ever, at the Oddfellows Hall, Ness, near Neston, Jack Roberts. Then there was the incomparable Alf Hassell. Alf was a legend in his own lifetime. He was a complete enigma. He shunned the white keys as though they were contaminated, concentrating solely on the blacks. Yet he could play any tune to the complete satisfaction of the most discerning ear.

As a vocalist however, this limitation put so many tunes outside my range that I could not work with him as many times as I would have liked. Nevertheless we did many memorable gigs together, notably a series at Moreton Picture House on Sunday evenings and many equally happy affairs as far apart as Liverpool and Holywell where Alf was extremely popular. Alf Hassell also holds a unique position at this stage in my life in that his was the first live band I ever sat and listened to.

I remember the occasion well. It was at the Town Liberal Hall in Claughton Road. I was fascinated by Alf's versatility — and also by the young lady providing the vocals. Her name was Betty Barnes and she must have been at least 5'10" tall. Her voice was as striking as her appearance, but what really struck me was the fact that she sang through a megaphone. This was about 10" long, black lacquered, with her monogram "B.B." in gold against the black.

This was the first and only time I saw a megaphone used. Shortly afterwards when I sang my first song at Ness near Neston, an enterprising young Radio Dealer from Livingstone Street, but whose shop was in Price Street, introduced the first Microphone into Birkenhead. The young man's name was Dick Jones and he hired the microphone out to local bands. The charge, I believe, was 7 shillings and sixpence.

I cannot claim to be the first vocalist to have used this microphone. That honour, as far as I can recollect, went to my predecessor with the Bill Owens band at Ness, a very fine vocalist called Johnny Conlan.

Incidentally, present-day "Groups" may be interested and probably amused, to know that Dick Jones Grampian Mike with its twin speakers which would be hung one on each wall halfway down the hall, pushed out 8 watts only. Compared with the ear splitting 100s of watts from each of the multiple speakers used today, our 8 watts appear ludicrous. However, the musicians, vocalists and the customers, considered our equipment quite adequate.

Among many other pianists with whom I had the pleasure of working at that time, were Les Sesford, Harry Middleton, Vernon Bissell, the Cooper brothers, Ken Williams, Wally Huston, etc. Lady pianists also figured prominently in the dance scene of the thirties. Lilly Lettis, a brilliant accompanist who, much against my will, persuaded me to play and sing "Olde Tyme" for which I shall be eternally grateful, for I loved the songs and Lil's inimitable piano playing. Another lady pianist with whom I worked regularly was Jean Platt.

Strangely enough, two very accomplished lady pianists with whom it was not my good fortune to sing, were Mary McKeown, née Pridgeon and Rita Farrell. Mary lived just a few doors from me in Patricia Avenue and Rita just off Hoylake Road, a few hundred yards away. .

Apart from local bands and pianists, I have been honoured to sing with Joe Loss, Teddy Joyces Canadians, The Four Aces, Bill Gregson at the Tower Ballroom, New Brighton, Jack Lee's orchestra with whom I sang a Sunday night season at the Floral Pavilion, New Brighton, the Grosvenor Hotel, Chester, orchestra, not forgetting Lord Leverhulme's hunt ball at Thornton Manor with Ron Baron and the 'Modernaires'. I was actually singing with Teddy Joyces Canadians at the Trocadero, Elephant and Castle, London, when war was declared. So ended my professional career before it had chance to take off. "C'est la guerre".

At most engagements we could count on at least one aspiring Bing Crosby or Anne Shelton to request to try their talents on the microphone. One gifted girl I recall was a Frances Gibson.

There was one, quite young, lady aspirant however, who, after a few bars, convinced me that she had that certain something which, to say the least, was different. It was a husky, unusual quality in her voice, but more importantly, a sense of timing and rhythm denied to most. This, and a general air of self-confidence and exuberance, gave her that plus factor. In one so young, this seemed to me to be a great portent for the future.

So it was that this particular girl, Enda Careful, not Edna, but Enda, found herself at 58, Patricia Avenue the following Sunday going through a few numbers with me.

She became a regular performer at local dances and also at troop concerts at venues such as St. George's and Picton Halls, Liverpool, where we performed regularly on Sunday evenings in the early days of the War.

This story has a strange sequel, in that I was lying on my bunk one Saturday afternoon in Army Barracks in Northern Ireland, from whence we were to disperse to southern England prior to "D" Day, when, above the usual barrack room clatter I heard over the radio, Harry Roy announcing a lady vocalist, "Eve Lombard". The first few bars were enough to convince me that this "Eve Lombard" was indeed my Enda Careful, a fact which I proudly proclaimed to the other occupants of the barrack room. My claim was greeted inevitably with "Rubbish!" — plus other unprintable obscenities.

Another who received his singing baptism at St. George's Hall in 1940, was my 12-year-old nephew, Terry Butler, who, kitted out with a Woolworths' Air Force forage hat, price 6d., sang to thousands of troops such rousing songs as "Lords of the Air", and "There'll always be an England." These numbers, sung in his boyish treble voice, brought the house down, time after time.

Terry is now a fine performer with a powerful voice which has no need of a microphone. He can also be seen regularly on the customer side of the bar in "Coronation Street", and he also made an appearance in "Boys from the Black Stuff". Ironically, in neither role is use made of his main asset — his singing voice.

THE BLITZ AND BIDSTON PARISH HALL

In my youth, and shortly after I was married, I led a dance band and our job on one particular night was to be at Bidston Parish Hall.

Our first proud home, after marriage, was 19, Thornton Street, and it was from there that we set out, my wife and I, to Bidston Hall.

The month was March, the year, 1941 — and it was just before I was called up for War service.

The Parish Hall was situated in a field, up a lane, which was opposite Bidston Parish Church. The field around the hall was bristling with anti-aircraft guns.

We had been playing and the crowds in the hall were enjoying themselves as usual, when suddenly the hall shook and the sound of the ack ack guns could be clearly heard above the music and chatter of the dancers.

In spite of the fact that the obvious implication was that bombers were close, the dancers, with very few exceptions, carried on. However, after a few more salvoes from the guns and bomb bursts getting ominously closer, we decided, and Jack Poval, the caretaker, agreed, that a wooden structure, with shrapnel raining down on the roof, was not exactly the ideal situation to be in. I therefore advised the dancers that, regretfully, we should abandon ship and make our way home.

My wife and I drove through the night along Hoylake Road and Laird Street in a canvas-topped Morris Minor, the sky brilliantly lit by the flares and the streets liberally covered with burning incendiary bombs.

On arrival at our home in Thornton Street, we immediately dived for cover under the stairs, our only shelter at that time. This we had already prepared with a mattress and meagre rations.

By this time things had really hotted up. Every explosion brought its inevitable damage or at least shake up and fright. At one time the gasometer at the bus depot behind Brassey Street had an incendiary through it and my brother-in-law, Teddy Sherlock, who lived at number 24, ran across to see if we were alright and to tell us that bodies were already being laid out along Norman Street. An Ariel mine had landed on the then comparatively new Avenue Cinema and had taken most of the roofs off houses from Mallaby Street along the line of streets towards Lansdowne Road.

Our own house was soot filled and roofless. It was not until morning light that the full impact of the night's events were brought home to us. The tragic loss of life was, of course, the first thing. Then there was the loss of homes, among them our own, particularly as this was our first home as newly-weds. There was a strange phenomenon regarding blast and its effects, whilst the damage to the cinema was a direct hit. Damage to the surrounding houses was caused by blast from this Ariel mine.

The after effects of blast must be seen to be believed. In our case, every metal object, pots, pans, etc., were twisted into grotesque shapes. No sculpture, however "way out", or modernistic, could hope to emulate it. Even stranger, if that is possible, was that the living room was covered with ladies new hats, presumably sucked through the air by the blast, from Nelsons, a ladies milliners in Laird Street, a quarter of a mile away.

With the realisation that our house was uninhabitable, came the equally disturbing thought that accommodation must be found and quickly. A hasty run around relatives left us in no doubt that we were all in the same boat.

Our saviour, or so we thought, was a fact forgotten in all of the turmoil. We were due to play that night at West Kirby. This event was to celebrate the 21st birthday of a member of a famous Merseyside Music House.

On arrival at the hall we were given quite an ovation for turning-up given the circumstances. In reply to this ovation I said that under these same circumstances, may we be allowed to sleep in the hall after the festivities were finished. This, we were assured, could and would be arranged.

The hall management, however, had other ideas, and as soon as we had packed up our instruments, we were instructed that we would have to leave.

My wife and I spent that night in a trench shelter dug out of the sands at West Kirby sandhills, bitterly cold, thoroughly miserable, but at least having the dubious satisfaction of hearing the bombers passing us by on their way to bomb Merseyside once more.

To revert to my reference to my good friend, Bill Collins, pianist and accordianist. Little did we know at that time that in a few years, a blond, curly-haired cherub of a boy, would emerge at Gautby Road, to be christened "Lewis". I suspect that this was after the great Lewis Stone, the band leader. Lewis's formative years were spent, unfortunately, without a mother. However, Bill took over both parental roles. A duty he undertook very seriously if in a somewhat unorthodox fashion.

On my infrequent visits to my parents, infrequent because my business took me all around the country, I always enquired about Bill, and his boy, Lewis. My mother's opinion of Lewis's upbringing was, to say the least, unfavourable. Typical of her remarks were, "That lovely little boy will never attain manhood. His father will kill him, either driving a motor cycle or on the firing range." Or later — "Playing in that group ("The Mojos") is far too much for a boy of his age."

That little blond, curly-haired boy, whose father was, according to my dear mother "Pushing him far too quickly through boyhood into adolescence and manhood, via motor cycles, rifles and other pursuits totally beyond a boy of his age", survived to become the T.V. star of the "Cuckoo Waltz", "The Professionals", the star of "Who Dares Wins", and many other shows, too numerous to mention.

My mother lived long enough to acknowledge the fact that Bill must have been correct after all, and to enjoy Lew's success.

Gautby Road could also boast another celebrity. Just a dozen or so doors away from the Collins's lived Ross McManus, trumpeter/vocalist with the Joe Loss Orchestra.

Since returning to Birkenhead, I have discovered among my newly acquired friends, and living in an adjacent road, Kay Mason, now Kay Roberts, vocalist with the Lew Stone Orchestra in 1936.

Chapter 4
LOCAL HEROES
Dixie Dean and other Characters

Without a shadow of a doubt, the most famous name to play for Wirral Railway F.C. was an ex railway man himself and the son of an engine driver whose engine literally passed the ground many times daily. The name — Billy Dean.

Nobody could ever have envisaged that Billy, or "Digsy" Dean, as he was called, would in a few short years be world famous as "Dixie" Dean of Everton and England.

On Bill Dean's sad death in 1980, the "Liverpool Echo", in memory of this great man, requested true stories from its readers in tribute to him. I was pleased to contribute the following:—

"The name Dixie Dean will always be synonymous with sportsmanship and goal scoring records, but in July 1929 Bill Dean added salesmanship to these attributes.

"My father, who was trainer to Wirral Railway F.C.; one of Bill's earlier amateur teams, brought the now great Everton and England player to my home to try to persuade my mother to allow me to play in a charity challenge tournament at St. Edward's Orphanage in Liverpool. The opposing teams were to be from Liverpool, Blackpool, Burnley and of course my home town, Birkenhead. This 'knock-out' tournament was a result of a difference of opinion between Louis Page of Burnley, "Tiny" Bradshaw of Liverpool, Frank O'Donnel of Blackpool and of course our own Bill Dean. Each was confident that a team from his town could beat any other. I was playing for Birkenhead and Cheshire boys, but my mother strongly objected to her 13½-year old, six stone, six pound son playing against men.

"It took two more visits and more blarney than I have heard from any professional salesman to win her over. The clincher was Bill's promise that although there were no medals to be won, he would personally give me one if I played.

"The tournament, which we won, took place on August 5th 1929 and my most vivid memory, apart from our victories, was when we stripped and Bill handed to me one of his England shirts to put on. Needless to say it dropped almost to my feet. Bill promptly folded it up and tied the folds around my middle with his belt.

"I got the medal, plus a signed studio photograph of Bill taken in his England shirt and sporting his 1926/27 international cap.

"The medal and photograph are still in my possession.

"The engraver made one mistake on the medal. It reads W. Houldin, Dixie Dean's XI. The fact is that it was a six-a-side tournament.

"I am afraid that my memory is a little hazy on the names of my team mates that day, but I believe that among them was my friend and fellow Birkenhead schoolboy, Sam Loudon, "Pudding" Johnson and Lou Griffiths. The pity of it is that no photographs were taken of the event."

Sis Kirby

Sis Kirby was noted in the Blocks for her "malapropisms", a word, incidentally, of which at that time, we were completely unaware. Sis, a large, childless lady, who lived in

"I" Block was completely oblivious to the fact that she was the source of so much amusement by her sayings. Typical examples of these gems would be "I get a lot of "compensation" on my windows", or "I was chased by a b---dy big "alteration" dog," or, during a busmen's strike, "If the drivers and "conjurers" don't take their uniforms back . . . ." etc.

Another example of Sis's eccentricity was when she bought herself a gold wristlet watch even though she could not tell the time. As children we soon cottoned on to this deficiency and of course at every opportunity we would ask Sis the time. She would make an exaggerated pretence at studying her watch and then she would extend her arm with the words "Look for yourself."

When Cecil Heydon, whose family lived next door to Sis, (and who incidentally, subsequently went on to play for New Brighton, Doncaster and Derby County, was five or six years old, we used to accompany our mothers and Sis to Wirral Railway football matches. Cecil was too small to look over the ledge around the stand and, as the story from my mother had it, kept up a continuous wail of "who's "yinning", mam?" In later years, as a professional footballer, he would have blushed to hear that story.

Ted Kirby, Sis's husband, had an allotment opposite "H" block in Ilchester Road. A feature of this was a bucket into which one's coppers were thrown for the bunches of rhubarb stacked alongside. I am told that the money collected was never short vis a vis the rhubarb stacked.

Whilst on the subject of Ilchester Road, mention must be made of other "Institutions" along there. Next in line to Kirby's was "Bucky" Hester's yard and stable followed by Rogerson's allotment.

At the top of the road and opposite to "A" Block was "Gan Yans" coal yard, later to be taken over by Tom Malone and Bill Ashley. The former made a name for himself as a player with Clydebank and Rangers in bonny Scotland.

In the opposite direction and over the railway bridge and on the ground where now stands Humber and Trent Streets, was Birkenhead' Nomads football ground, known to all as Quinney's field. Beyond that, and down to Beaufort Street, or the "Dock Road" as we call it, was an enclosed area containing old life boats, etc.

In the corner of this enclosure and directly opposite the graving dock entrance, was a wooden hall housing Mr Belsey's Sea Scouts. Mr Belsey, small in stature but big in heart, taught many boys the rudiments of sailing in this hall and sailing in the West Float. Many boys owe a deep debt of gratitude to Belsey and for his work.

Annie Doyle

Annie Doyle lived in the top lobby in "G" Block with her mother, Rose Ann and brother, Jimmy. She was a hard working, God fearing woman who followed the very tough trade of Scrap Metal Merchant.

Her yard was on a boarded-up triangle of land at the corner of Tyrer Street and Stanley Road. Annie worked extremely hard and long for each penny she earned.

Unfortunately the local lads were not averse to pulling the occasional 'fast one' on her. She would be induced to step outside to inspect some item brought for sale. The sellers' accomplices, meanwhile, would have climbed the fence at the rear, and would be busily engaged in throwing out a selection of her stock to their friends on the back side of the yard. After a fair interval, these accomplices would walk around to the front and calmly proceed to sell back to Annie her own metal. I cannot remember hearing of her ever discovering the deception.

My knowledge of Jimmy Doyle was of a man afflicted by a disease resulting in a shuffling gait, and almost incoherent speech. We were told that as a younger man, Jim was a tall, handsome, intelligent and very competent marine engineer. On one of his trips across the Atlantic he became engaged to an American lady. On a subsequent trip to America this young lady decided that things were over between them. The news so shocked Jimmy that he had a mild stroke of which his present condition was the result. Fortunately the affliction had not affected his brain which was **active** and shrewd.

A favourite game among the "Blocks" boys, 90% of whom were golf addicts, and caddies, was a gambling, putting game, usually in Royden's field, where now stands Patricia Avenue and the right-hand side of Gautby Road houses. Three holes were laid out in a triangle and odds were laid by Jimmy Doyle on his assessment of the punters' putting ability. These games would go on sometimes for hours. Money was won and lost, and also, indirectly, many fine putters emerged. Most certainly many of these caddies, as a result of this practice, became better golfers than the men they caddied for. This was hardly surprising as it was often said that all Dock Cottage lads were born with a golf club in their hands.

Certain it was that opportunities to learn the game through caddying were there in abundance when one considers the proximity of the "Blocks" to the West Cheshire, Bidston, Leasowe, Wallasey, Wirral Ladies, Prenton, and, a little further out, Hoylake, courses. It seemed natural, therefore, that the boys and youths of the area would take up caddying and become artisan golfers at some of these clubs, notably West Cheshire.

Ike Carrington

Ike Carrington lived with his family, — wife, sons, Dave and Billy, and his daughter, in Stanley Road, opposite to the Tapestry Works. His business was pig farming. This he carried on in his piggery, which was situated in Gautby Road, beyond the older type houses on the left. The back of his pig farm would be where Townsend Street houses now stand.

Very often, as boys, we would watch Ike at work, mucking out, hosing down, feeding etc. One day word spread around like wildfire that Ike was being very naughty with his pigs. The boy who instigated this rumour was willing to bet his week's pocket money that he had witnessed this shocker with his own eyes. In his words, "Dogs do it."

It was a year or so before Ike's reputation was restored to its impeccable level. The explanation was provided by a country boy who informed us that this "Naughty act", so called, was a pig farmer's accepted method of ascertaining whether or not the sow was in season and would be receptive to the boar. The farmer would attempt to lie along the sow's back. If she was "Ready" he would be allowed to stay. If she was not, the unfortunate man would be deposited on to the farm yard floor, with all that that means.

So much for circumstantial evidence and perfectly innocent Ike Carrington.

Ellen Purcell's Shop in 'I' Block

At 4 or 5 years old, I was unaware that, with the exception of Sundays, when the whole family paraded for church, days bore names.

I was, however, very well aware that one day was very special. On the evening of this day my father would produce, as if by magic, 25 or 30 shillings, which he would present to my mother. Eventually, after a great deal of hopping about in anticipation, my sister, my brother, and I, would be handed one penny each.

This weekly windfall was cherished, not only for its exchange value, but more importantly, because it was the metaphorical key which opened the door to the enchanted shop wherein lived old Ellen Purcell. Of all women, and at that age my world seemed to be almost exclusively peopled by women, old Ellen was the most fascinating, the most awesome.

There were many small shops in the "Blocks" where cleanliness, civility, and a more varied selection of sweets would be on offer. Ellen's shop fell far short on all counts but one, the strange, almost thrilling, feeling that only entry into old Ellen's' could evoke.

This was no ordinary shop. The only concession to convention was an ancient pair of scales on an equally ancient table which, on reflection, I suspect was tilted in Ellen's favour.

The imperious lady herself sat in an old rocking chair next to a black-grated fire. Bracketed to the wall above her head was an incandescent mantled gas jet which cast an eerie glow over the figure beneath.

From her buttoned-up booted feet to her wrinkled white chin, she was a study in sombre black, — the voluminous skirt, the pleated blouse with the high ruffed collar, seemingly supporting the silver-haired head.

Always, close to Ellen's hand, was a long cane, which could reach from her chair to the very limited space where you were obliged to stand, the whole 9-foot by 9-foot room being an Aladdin's cave of 'goodies', piled, box upon box, bottle upon bottle — "Gobstoppers", "Aniseed balls", "Liquorice sticks", the list seemed endless.

Ellen's opening remarks, "What do you want?" — "How much have you got?" — barked out in stentorian tones, would never have won a diploma in a school of salesmanship, but was most certainly an aid to decision making.

Having stated your choice, Ellen, with unerring accuracy, would tap, with her cane, one of the multitude of boxes or jars with which she was completely surrounded. The next tap would be on the top of your head. This was the unspoken command to deliver the chosen box or jar to her side.

After weighing or counting, the old lady would produce a piece of newspaper which she would, as if by magic, transform into a cone and into which your chosen goodies disappeared.

I remember always hoping that some boy or girl would enter and ask for paraffin. This was because Ellen would be obliged to leave her seat, something the childish mind believed she could never do. True the paraffin tank was only a yard or so away, but the act was a ritual in itself. That few feet took her behind what was the back kitchen door, to the tank. You were obliged to take your can to her. Then would come the barked order to get back to your place. Whilst serving the appropriate measure into the can, Ellen would issue a stream of commands — "Keep your hands in your pockets" — "Put that down, I can see you," etc. Although she was behind the door I could never be sure that she did not possess the power to see through it.

Wise old Ellen must have realised that I had sensed that behind that fierce facade lay a heart of gold — and maybe there was a feeling of regret that she had never married and been blessed with little customers of her own. Suffice it to say she was kind enough to leave to me a Victorian five-shilling piece when she died. Dated 1900, the coin is in my collection of souvenirs.

Wally Thom

Boxing celebrities may not figure as prominently as footballers or golfers in the history of the "Blocks", but one man's record amply compensates for this imbalance.

Wally Thom was born to Nellie Thom, née Lawton, in a flat under ours in "G" Block, "up our lobby." This, unassuming, gentle boy was to become British and Empire Welterweight champion, and later, on retirement, a class 1, highly respected referee.

Years after leaving the Dock Cottages and living 150 miles away, I brought my family to visit my parents in Patricia Avenue. As a treat, I took my son, Barry, aged 10 years, to meet my dear friend, Wally, at his home. Wally wrapped the Lonsdale belt around my son's waist and then paid me the most unexpected compliment, which was, and I quote, "If I had not climbed the whippet track railings to watch your father training, I may never have got the bug which led to my winning this belt."

Considering that my short career was as a 12 shillings and sixpence "six rounder" it would not even merit comment but for Wally's remark, so typical of this great sportsman.

It was my dubious pleasure when on business in Newcastle on Tyne many years ago, to take Wally to Newcastle General hospital to have his eyebrow stitched after being butted by Vincent O'Kine. Johnny Campbell, Wally's manager, learning that I was staying overnight in the city, invited me to view the fight at St. James' Hall.

Wally was a credit to Johnny, to the sport, the town and the "Blocks" wherein he was born. His untimely end at 53 was a grievous loss to his childhood sweetheart wife, his family, friends and to the sport he graced to the end.

The Cobbler

Eddie Ithel was one of almost extinct breed, a Cobbler. His work shop was no bigger than the space taken up by two 'phone boxes and was simply a boarded-up corner of Annie Doyle's scrap metal yard. This was situated on the corner of Tyrer Street and Stanley Road.

Across the corner and under the small window was fastened a 12-inch wide by 3-inch thick plank which served as Eddie's bench. To this was fastened a strong metal ring, covering a hole into which he slotted the "last" appropriate to the size and type of shoe he happened to be working on. Unlike the stapled soles and heels made of some synthetic material used today, Cobblers stripped soles of pure leather, levelled up the base and then cut and shaped a sole of natural leather from a huge sheet which they proceeded to nail on as only an expert cobbler could.

Behind Eddie's bench was barely enough room for a large box which contained his lasts, nails, knives and the boots awaiting repair.

This box also served as a seat for myself and my pal, Sammy Loudon. Eddie seemed particularly fond of us because he was a great lover of sport and Sam and I played for our respective schools, and together for Birkenhead schoolboys.

So we would sit and listen to tales of **real** footballers and boxers while the pile of repaired shoes would grow. One piece of equipment I have neglected to mention and one which was an essential, albeit the cheapest implement in the place, was a loop of clothes line. This would be placed behind the heel, the other end of the loop hanging loosely about 6 inches from the floor. By placing his foot into the bottom of the loop and bearing-down, Eddie would pull the shoe, via the heel, very tightly and firmly on to the last.

Mrs Ithel was a very attractive lady and would very often leave her baby son Max in the "shop". Max would sit for hours among the leathers, boots and tools quite content, while his father would stand, his mouth filled with nails, belting a sole or heel onto a shoe. He always finished the nailing with a distinctive pattern, which, in retrospect, I suppose was his individual trade mark.

I am sure that my friend, Sam, would agree that the hours we spent listening and talking to Eddie Ithel — cobbler, philosopher, and gentleman — sometimes by the light of an oil lamp, were educational, enjoyable and memories to be treasured.

Eddie's extremely placid nature, his acute sense of humour, coupled with his ability to regale us with his stories, never condescendingly told or in bad taste, endeared him to me as did few outside of my own family circle.

Ike Grey

The largest character, in a literal as well as story sense, was Ike Grey. I would guess Ike to be 16 to 18 stones of gentle, mild-mannered, hard-working, hard-drinking, giant.

The mental picture I still carry, is of Ike walking up Ilchester Road from the docks area, having done a hard day's work. His cap would be slightly askew, his thumbs in trouser tops, a great paunch overhanging the trousers and sometimes a couple of lower shirt buttons undone to reveal a a prominent navel. So much for week days.

On Saturday and possibly on Sunday nights another facet of Ike's nature would be revealed. On his way up Stanley Road from the "Blood Tub", uninhibited and happy, invariably supported, if such is the word, by his beloved Violet, all 7 to 8 stones of her, he would be singing some unintelligible song and smiling the smile of a man who had nothing more to ask of life. She, with the look of a devoted wife, would be content to assist, morally if not physically, in her weekly duty of seeing her Ike safely home.

On one of these Violet-assisted journeys from that fountain of joy, the "Blood Tub", somebody, or something, upset our jovial giant. Result — Ike standing in the middle of "B" Block, 10-30 to 11 p.m. demanding retribution from someone — anyone, for the wrong, real or imagined, which he had suffered.

News of an impending punch-up would spread around the blocks as Tom Toms around a jungle, consequently within minutes, quite a sizeable proportion of the Blocks population were crowded into "B" Block, plus the onlookers from storeys high, looking through their windows onto the arena beneath, all waiting to see who the lion heart would be to take up Ike's challenge to the world.

The interruption, rather than challenge, came in the shape of "Curly", one of our local bobbies. "Curly" pushed his way through the crowd in an effort to placate Ike. Sober, Ike would have greeted him as any Blocks' resident always did, as a trusted friend. Unfortunately the officer may have pushed that little bit too hard, or maybe Ike was just that little bit too 'far gone' to appreciate the policeman's motives. Be that as it may, Ike pushed him away, causing him to lose his balance and his dignity.

Our friendly "bobby" stood, calmly removed his helmet and his jacket, handed them to a spectator in the certain knowledge that they would be returned to him unharmed, and told Ike to prepare for action.

Although Ike outweighed his opponent by a couple of stones, his condition proved his undoing and it became evident very soon that Ike must surely succumb. This he did gracefully.

"Curly" retrieved his helmet and jacket, donned both, and helped the now quiet and resigned Ike, with his ever faithful Violet, up the lobby to his home.

Ike did not lose face, and the "Scuffer" (colloquial word for policeman), as was usual in those days, calmly went about his business.

If my recollection of such events and of uniformed friends of the period is correct, then that particular incident would not have even been entered in the officer's little book.

Jim McSherry

Mrs McSherry, always called Mrs Sherry, had three daughters. One was a nun. The other two were called Lyn and Maggie. I was unaware of the existence of a son until word spread around the blocks that Jimmy Sherry was home from America.

We learned also that Jimmy, in the tradition of blocks' boys, was a golfer. In this instance he was a golfer with a difference — a trick golfer.

Jim appeared at the one time world famous Argyle theatre in Birkenhead. The culmination of his act was to drive golf balls off his sister, Maggie's, nose. To the best of my knowledge Maggie's nose remained intact.

The Gordons and Sherlocks

Up the bottom lobby in "K" Block, lived a man who, in those days of sparsity and no Ministry hand-outs, was determined to use his brains to find ways to feed his family. Tom Gordon contrived to make a few 'bob' by making an ingenious little "Moaning Minnie". This consisted of a strip of wood about 5-inches and 1½-inches by half an inch. Along each edge Tom would gouge out notches about one inch apart. Through a hole at one end was threaded a 3-feet length of string knotted at the hole.

The proud owner would proceed to swing this simple device around his or her head at great speed. The result would be a strange moaning sound. The cost of the "Moaning Minnie" was a half-penny.

Today's children must derive an immense amount of pleasure from their electronic games and computers, but Tom Gordon's "Hummers" kept many Dock Cottages children very happy until theirs was eventually lost or had disintegrated.

The Sherlocks, also up this lobby, were a quiet, unassuming family, mainly boys. One eventually became a "Bobby" on Bidston Hill. Another one also joined the Parks

Department and ended his working days at Victoria Park. He and his wife are as happy today as when they met as members of the Salvation Army.

Up the next lobby and in the same block lived Mrs Love. She was a very gentle old lady who kept Pekingese dogs. A thoroughbred dog, of any breed was a unique sight in our part of the world.

The same lobby housed Bev, known to all as "Biff", Taylor, just one more of the many artisan golfers in the blocks. The Calveley family also lived above.

The ground floor shop in the next lobby was owned by "Lump" and Annie Fowler. We were not to know then that Annie Fowler was a member of the great Rugby League family, the "Lawtons" of Widnes. The Lawton's boys, in later years, played for Widnes and Great Britain on many occasions.

The Magic Box

The "Bells" lived in "K" Block. Mr Bell was a sea-going engineer with a lovely wife and two very nice children. There was the young boy, Billy, later to become a policeman, and Eunice.

"Mr Bell has a box that talks." Even a silly 9-years old girl could expect nothing but derision from a sophisticated 7-years old brother on being told this ridiculous story.

The year was 1922 and my sister was a regular visitor to the Bells' house as a baby sitter. Her story, so breathlessly told that I had to frequently exhort her to slow down, was, that Mr Bell had a black box which could talk and make music. He simply placed what looked like black, hollowed out, power puffs over each ear, twiddled a knob, and voices or music came through.

Previous visits to the Bells had been the prerogative of my sister, May, now, partly to confound her cynical brother, but, I suspect, because she was more than a little apprehensive, the invitation for her next visit was extended to me.

Never in my seven long years was I so shocked, thrilled, intrigued and scared, all at the same time, as on that evening when the pads were placed over my ears, and music, seemingly from nowhere, filtered through.

Weeks later, when our secret threatened to explode from within us, we confided in our parents. The mystery simply deepened when my father said, "Oh, that must be one of those 'Cat's Whisker' wirelesses."

Truly, a room containing a box which talked, sang, and played music through "cats' whiskers" must be a magical room.

45

Chapter 5
BEYOND THE "BLOCKS"

TAPESTRY WORKS

We were not aware of the fact as children, but Arthur H. Lee's Tapestry Works in Stanley Road, were world-famous. We were blissfully unaware that what went on behind the brick and corrugated iron walls, culminated in a product which adorned the walls of some of the most famous buildings and ships in the world. The Company was founded in Britain by A.H. Lee in 1888 and in America in 1903.

The aim was to create beautiful tapestries and furnishing fabrics in an age when design was suffering from mechanisation. Handwork played a very prominent part in the firm's products which included Crewel embroidering, hand needlework and hand-blocked Jacquard woven tapestries. To this range of unsurpassed tapestries, plain cloths, damasks and hand embroideries was added also one of the finest collections of chintzes and linens available anywhere in the world.

Lees could reproduce any design, stitching or colouring, of any period in history, even to the colours mellowed by centuries of time.

At the time of closure, A.H. Lee's proud claim was that the third and fourth generation of the family still actively controlled the company worldwide.

In March, 1965, the internationally famous American Company JOFA Inc: was acquired by Lee.

If only we Dock Cottagers had been aware of the empire that this gentleman, who walked into his building so unobtrusively controlled, we would have striven to join this vast undertaking. Alas! we were only aware of that tiny part encompassed by the walls of Stanley Road.

As far as I was concerned the Tapestry Works claim to fame was that they seemed to have selected all the nicest girls from the North End to work for them. Secondly, and probably the most important factor to me as a child, was that old Mr Lee provided a Magic Lantern show every Thursday at 5.30 p.m. for the local children. This remarkable, white-haired, goatee-beared philanthropist, would stand behind a large cabinet, smoke issuing from a vent in the top, which projected slides onto a large white screen.

The show always commenced with an illustrated bible story with a narration by Mr Lee. This would be followed by a couple of primitive slide cartoons. This was the highlight of our week and one which generated excitement to the heights, and for which we queued for what seemed an eternity. The accommodation was so limited and the demand so great, that it was inevitable that there would be many disappointed clients. Some there were who took this philosophically and played elsewhere. There were those, however, who did not accept their loss in the Christian spirit which the very generous Mr Lee would have liked. The favourite outlet for this frustration was to use the side of the corrugated iron-sheeted building as a deafening drum. A stone held firmly in one hand and rubbed along the corrugations from one end of the building to the other, produced a noice inside, akin to a great thunderstorm.

To provide the show, this remarkable gentleman, Mr Lee, apart from giving of his own time and trouble involved in arranging the programme, had, in addition, to pay staff overtime to arrange the seating and to supervise the boisterous crowd of youngsters, who, in a fever of excitement and anticipation, would be shouting and pushing, jealously guarding their position in the queue, or their seats in the hall.

Today's children would have chocolate, sweets or crisps to take into their place of entertainment, we in stark contrast, had a jam butty. Failing that, the naughtier element among us would, before queueing, make our way to the "plantation", a series of allotments now built upon and taking in Harding, Mason and Goodwin Avenues, topped by Hoylake Road. I am afraid that many hardworking allotment holders would discover a few holes where once had been turnips. We, for some unknown reason, called these "chowows". I never found out from whence this strange name derived. However, our "chowows" would be scraped and eaten with relish during Mr Lees' narration.

The caretaker, Mr Critten, and his family, lived in a wooden bungalow adjacent to the office. He was followed by Ron Hayden, whose sister was a long serving employee.

Another achievement by this great man, Mr Lee, was the establishment of a camp at Dyserth, near to Prestatyn. I was fortunate enough to be chosen to attend this camp for a couple of weeks. My mother gave me threepence to spend. This had gone by the end of the first three days on a card and stamp. The message read, "Dear Mother, I am homesick. Please send my bus fare home."

The name "Arthur Lee" will always be revered by people who were privileged to work for him, and by the hundreds of children who were entertained by this gentleman with no hope of reward or even verbal thanks.

Among the many notable orders executed by this unique company was one for 40,000 square yards of floor covering for the state rooms of the "Queen Elizabeth," a hand-embroidered love seat for Hussein of Jordan and a huge, hand-embroidered, carpet, a wedding gift to his daughter from the president of the giant "Chrysler" Corporation of America.

On the occasion of the first visit to Birkenhead of Her Majesty Queen Elizabeth on May 3rd, 1950, the Borough presented to her Majesty, a fire screen, the embroidered Crewel work panel, the worsted damask in the back and all the cord and trimmings being made by A.H. Lee at the Stanley Road Tapestry Works. The "Crewel work" embroidery was of "long and short" stitch and French knots, producing a wealth of interest in the way each stitch is laid in turn, to twist or radiate, promoting the shape and form of leaf and petal.

Among the names to be remembered among the many fine people who worked virtually to the end of this company, are Gladys Rimmer, Emily Reid, the Gaunt sisters and Dolly Blythe. Present on the photograph of the last stitch being inserted by Emily Reid are Mr Christopher Lee, Mr Stephen Lee, Mr Michael Lee and Mr Lefeurve.

One wonders what Mr Lees' thoughts would be if he were alive today to view the site of his world-famous factory, now a supermarket.

"THE KNACKERS YARD"

In Beaufort Road and opposite to the end of Ilchester Road was an establishment known officially as "Wirral Refinery", but locally as "The Knackers Yard." Here horses, which in those days were as numerous on the roads as cars, were brought after being slaughtered, or killed accidentally.

The process at the refinery was to retrieve everything of value from the carcass, bones, hoofs, and meat. I understand that glue was one of the important by-products.

My most powerful memory of this yard was of the overpowering stench. Another was of writhing heaps of maggots in piles as high as three feet around the building.

Across waste land on the same side of the road as the refinery and opposite to the Graving Dock Hotel was the depot for what was then a famous name in petrol, "Pratts". From "Pratts" and occupying the rest of the land to the Dock wall was, and is still, the Vacuum Oil Company. This company had their own tankers, sailing regularly from America to berth and discharge oil at this site.

From the Vacuum berth and up to the then "Penny Bridge", was "Cubbin's" Shipyard. They were barge builders and small ship repairers. Reas Tugs were prominent customers. Old Mr Cubbins could always be seen in the yard actively engaged in running the business. To describe Mr Cubbins would be to describe George Bernard Shaw, for he was his double.

The docks system ended at this yard. The Penny Bridge, then simply a permanent road bridge, separated it from the Wallasey Pool, at that time a stretch of grass banked water.

Many Dock Cottages' men and youths worked here. My own brother-in-law, Teddy Sherlock, served his time as a shipwright in the yard.

ALBERT INDUSTRIAL SCHOOL

In Corporation Road and in that area bounded by Miriam Place and Lincoln Street, stood a massive building behind a high brick wall. This was known to us as "The Albert Industrial School." The official title was "The Prince Albert Memorial Industrial School."

The building, erected at a cost of £5,000, was designed to accommodate 100 boys. Those admitted were adjudged to be in need of care or had been committed under the Industrial Schools Act, for some misdemeanour.

Sir William Jackson was the benefactor who bore the cost of the project. The school opened in 1863 and continued its excellent work until closure in 1924.

The boys' uniform consisted of a navy blue fisherman type jersey, or "ganzey" as we called it then, corduroy trousers down to the knee and thick navy blue stockings to just below the knee. The boots were of the old army type complete with studded soles and heels.

Opposite the school and extending from Lincoln Street to Buccleugh Street and down to the railway, was a field used by the school and also by local football clubs, including Lansdowne F.C.

At the Buccleugh Street/Corporation Road corner of the field was a small group of stables. One of these was owned by Billy Hill, a local bookie, owner of a racehorse called "Black Lion" which was a familiar sight being run around the field on the end of a 50-foot leather lead or strap. Another stable housed "Halliwell", the Laird Street butcher's, horse and trap.

It was in the course of a conversation with Mr Tom Beacall, father to a well-known "H" Block Dock Cottages family, at the time of the talk, in his mid-nineties, and living in Hoylake Road, that Mr Beacall informed me that he had been an Albert Industrial School boy.

The boys from the school were trained in industrial and nautical skills rather than in academic subjects and would invariably find jobs in shipyards or as seamen. Mr Beacall himself became a crew member of the White Star liner "Cedric" sailing out of Liverpool. He had a fund of stories about life on the "Cedric" and similar liners, but the most intriguing was the one he related to me about meeting a "Cedric" shipmate ashore in Liverpool, the crew having been paid off at the end of the voyage. The man asked Tom if he would be signing on for the next voyage. Tom countered with, "Why not?" His friend then informed him that the Company had a new ship due for her maiden voyage and that she would be paying £9.10-shillings per month against the £7 per month earned on the "Cedric". Tom was all for the idea until he was told that the vessel would be sailing out of Southampton. — It must be borne in mind that at the time of this incident, communications were primitive by today's standards. Few people owned even the most basic radio equipment, whereas today, via at least three branches of what we term 'the Media', television, radio and telephone, we know what is happening anywhere in the world almost as it happens. In those days news could take days, even weeks to percolate through. Likewise with travel. People seldom moved more than a few miles from home. Some Birkonians had not even crossed the water to Liverpool or Liverpudlians to Wirral. So it was that Tom Beacall, although a frequent visitor as a crew man to countries on the other side of the world, was reluctant to travel to Southampton by train, even for the extra couple of pounds per month, quite a sum at that time.

Thomas Henry Beacall lived to 99 years of age. His mate who made the journey to Southampton drowned on that maiden voyage. The ship — the ill-fated "Titanic."

48

WIRRAL RAILWAY F.C.

The leading amateur team in Wirral, and possibly in Cheshire, was Wirral Railway F.C. The ground was situated over the railway bridge at Bridge Road, down to Beaufort Road, then at right angles to a point about 15 yards short of the Graving Dock Hotel. Right angles again to the iron railed railway boundary line which then followed the line up to the Bridge Road start.

The whole ground, with the exception of the railway iron railings, was enclosed by an 8-foot, close-boarded fence. Although it was an amateur team, one paid for admission, which is indicative of the standard of football played and the status of the club.

Behind the fence at the Beaufort Road Graving Dock pub side of the ground, and running back to Ilchester Road, was Mr Rose's "Piggery". It was hardly an appropriate name for a pig breeder, but "Mr Rose" it was.

At the railway end and with its back overlooking the railway opposite Dock Station, was a large "grand stand". Under the stand were store rooms containing all the necessary ground keeping equipment, plus nets, goal posts, line markers, etc. Above, and up a flight of steps were changing rooms, — home, visitors and referees, — a committee and "social" room and the usual amenities.

Fronting these rooms was a wide verandah running the length of the building. This was the V.I.P.s viewing area. Apart from the usual visiting and home committee men, there was also the regular women's section of the club. Among the 'ever presents' were Mrs Jack Lewis and Mrs Ainslie, sisters to the Higgins brothers, Mick and Frank, Mrs Hayden, Sis Kirby, Gert Mumford, née Sutton, and other players' wives and girl friends. Another ever present was my mother who was honorary kit washer to the team as well as wife to the trainer.

As I have stated, this was no ordinary amateur team. Clubs from first, second and third divisions, plus Rangers and Clydebank in the Scottish league, fielded products of Wirral Railway F.C. Such names as Billy Fogg, Huddersfield Town; Frank Higgins, New Brighton; Tom Malone, Rangers and Clydebank, etc.

The ground occupied what are now Tyne and Tees Streets bounded by the Graving Dock Hotel, Beaufort Road to Wallasey Bridge Road, top and bottom.

When Wirral Railway F.C. regrettably folded up, the ground became a whippet racing track. In the area there was a square, floor boarded area, possibly a collecting ring for the dogs. Suffice to say that I had severed my connection with the Conway boxing club and, with my father's assistance, converted this area for training. At each session I had an audience of boys who used to climb the boards, which surrounded the square, to hang on by their arms and elbows to watch my routines.

As this unit was open to the elements, I transferred my bags and other equipment to the loft over a stable which was situated behind the Graving Dock Hotel, (Murphy's) in Beaufort Street.

It was here that one evening in the middle of a punch bag session, the floor flaps opened and two boys' heads appeared. They wanted to know if I would teach them to box. After one or two refusals, I finally agreed to their request. It became evident after a few weeks that one of the boys was improving at a much greater rate than his pal. This became so apparent that the lesser talented boy stopped coming.

The problem now was to find a sparring partner for my protege, Tommy O'Reily. Meanwhile I, as my father had done for me, knelt in front of the boy attempting to spar with him.

The time arrived when I considered that I must advise the boy that I could no longer help him and that his future lay in joining an amateur boxing club where I would not be allowed to participate.

The happy ending was that Tommy took my advice, and at a future date it gave me great pleasure to read in the national press — Thomas O'Reily, Birkenhead — 7 stone champion of Great Britain — 1936/37. Then again, the following year 1937/38 — Thomas O'Reily — Birkenhead — 8 stone, 7 pounds, schoolboy champion of Great Britain. A very gratifying end to a reluctant beginning.

A few years later I was to meet my pupil again. This time he was resplendent in a Flying Officer's uniform. He was on a short leave and he was all of 12½ stones of muscle.

It so happened that I had changed my sport to weight lifting at the insistence of a group of men who, in return for the use of their equipment and room in Holt's Club, Ashville Road, expected me to teach them the rudiments of boxing.

My weight lifting friends, hearing of my meeting with my ex pupil exhorted me to persuade Tommy to box an exhibition with me at their rooms. They failed to appreciate that I had not had a glove on for a couple of years and our young Flying Officer was boxing for the R.A.F. and was at least 2½ stones heavier than I was. The result was a foregone conclusion. My age and his weight and fitness proved an insurmountable combination.

The following Sunday after Mass, Mrs O'Reily made our gallant Flying Officer apologise for giving me the finest "shiner" I ever had. In her words, "There's gratitude for you."

VULCAN STREET

Although not of the "Blocks", we always considered streets around the periphery, or within hailing distance, housed our adopted "cousins".

The closest to us in this sense was, I should say, Vulcan Street. Maybe this was because of the large, closely knit families, reminiscent of the "Blocks" families, who lived there.

The most prominent among these families, for a variety of reasons, were the Parkers. The girls I knew not at all, but the boys I grew to know very well. I learned to respect them for their mode of living, hard working, respectable demeanour and impeccable dress. If you add to this, affable and gregarious natures then you had the Parkers. Ray Parker and I later served apprenticeships together in the same factory before he decided to seek his fortune in Rhodesia. Happily for me, after too many years, Ray returned to his home town and it was my pleasure to renew acquaintance. Regrettably, Ray passed away in 1984. Ray's brother, Bill, I meet fairly often and we always exchange fond reminiscences of our youth.

Vulcan Street corner, at Laird Street, was the meeting place for the boys of Vulcan Street, which is, incidentally, less than 50-yards from the Laird Street shop of the mother of the late, Dixie Dean.

Grouped on this corner, more often than not, were the Saunders boys. Harold played for Birkenhead Schoolboys with me. His brother, George, also played for the town and subsequently for Everton. Ron Saunders, Manager of Aston Villa is a member of this family.

LUNT'S BAKERY

On the corner of Stanley Road and opposite to St. James' Church, stood Lunt's cake and confectionery shop. The gateway to the huge bakery at the rear, was a few yards down Stanley Road. The yard housed a dozen or so large vans. They were green with "LUNTS" in a gold colour across the sides and back. These vans were reversed up to a long loading platform where bread, cakes, etc. were loaded from morning until late afternoon.

A great boon to the local populace, was the weekly sale of Lunt's "Stallers", pronounced with a short 'a', not a long one as in "Stawlers".

On one evening a week, I believe Thursdays, the locals would queue along the back wall of Stanley Road. Here we would wait until a hatch in the wall was opened, and on presentation of a couple of coppers, we would receive a large bag of stale, but nevertheless edible, and very welcome, cakes.

In later years, when I was maybe 12 and a half years old, I was to be very grateful to the manageress of the shop on the corner. I was grateful to Miss Hines on two counts. Firstly, she gave me a Saturday job delivering cakes to local shops. The trays were slotted into an attractively-boxed handcart, half-a-dozen trays at a time. For this I was paid 2/- (10-pence), working from 9 a.m. until 4 p.m. This ensured a regular weekly income for my mother, as opposed to the uncertainty of success at caddying. — Secondly, when I was chosen to play football for the school or the town or the county, Miss Hines allowed herself to be persuaded to allow me the time off. If the game was for the town or the county, this meant all day, but my 2/- was still there.

The great persuader was our maths master, Mr O'Donnell, and I am still unaware whether it was that the kindly Miss Hines covered for me or whether the late Roger O'Donnell did not himself hand over the 2/- to be paid to me. Alas, I will never know.

BIDSTON HILL

Nowadays children's arranged trips to the continent and beyond, are considered part of their education, and they have become quite blasé about their travels. Our 1920s trips, by comparison, must evoke great merriment, maybe even derision, if ever parents recount the stories. The modern educationalist would rate their value degrees below zero. Our rating then was sky high. No money, special clothing or luggage was necessary. Our list of necessities was short and inexpensive.

Item 1: A large lemonade bottle filled with water.
If very lucky, a packet of lemonade powder to flavour it, costing half-a-penny.
Item 2: A packet of newspaper-wrapped jam butties.
Item 3: A rubber, or tennis, ball.
Item 4: The will to stay out all day and chase, or be chased, around Bidston Hill, or, as we called it, "Biddy" Hill, and Pine Woods.

The windmill, the observatory, and the lighthouse, never ceased to hold enchantment for us as children.

Some reports from today's children regarding their trips to Paris, Boulogne, and all points east and west, would suggest to me that our "Biddy Hill" days were more productive, certainly more enjoyable, than theirs.

HOLY CROSS

Our Lady's parish, of which we were members, was swiftly spreading beyond its original parochial boundaries. It was decided therefore to introduce a new parish into the Bidston area. In their wisdom the church authority appointed a Father Lowery to minister to this new off-shoot.

The worthy priest was a tall, gangling figure whose trouser bottoms were always frayed and shabby. This was not unusual among the clergy of the day as they were entirely dependent upon the generosity of their flock. The average workers' earnings were low, if any at all. It follows that the offerings would therefore be low.

The new parish started without a church. Mass was celebrated in the bedroom of a house in Gautby Road opposite Harding Avenue.

The next move was to the Catholic Church in Flaybrick Hill Cemetery. Access to this church for Dock Cottagers was a right turn at Perrin Hall in Tollemache Road into the lane running around what we knew as "The Nanny Goat Mountains," — (actually the rock foundation upon which stands St. James' hospital, in those days called the Fever hospital. The path led to the cemetery gates and on to the small church.

As can be imagined, the church contained just the bare essentials. Seating was on a first come, first served, basis. The unlucky ones, or maybe those who chose this means of expiating their transgressions, would kneel on rough coconut matting which covered the floor. The hard squares of the matting left waffle-like indentations on the knees.

One steady source of income for the parish was the 6d "Snowball". These events were organised on a family rota basis. The "knees up", for that is really what a "Snowball" was, usually took place on a Sunday evening in a different house each time. A wind-up gramophone, some 78 R.P.M. records, a cup of tea, a slice of cake and a good jig, all in a tiny 9-foot by 9-foot room. The result could be a donation of 10-shillings, or more, to parish funds. Ten shillings could buy quite a lot in the '20s so the organiser was happy, the customers were satisfied, and the parish was 10/- better off.

Father Cavanagh was the next incumbent. His predecessor had been of a rather sombre nature and tall. Father Cavanagh was very much a contrast. He was jolly, one could almost say extrovert, and squarely built.

It seemed no time at all before a plot of land, bounded by Challis Street, Hoylake Road and Gautby Road, had been acquired. The men of the parish then proceeded to build what eventually became a corrugated iron church to be known as Holy Cross.

Father Cavanagh was not content just to watch his church taking shape. On most days he could be seen trundling a wheelbarrow, and at lunch break his would be the order for drinks in the "Ham and Eggs" pub for the men. The official name of the pub is "The Bidston Hotel."

By the time another great character, Father Campbell, came along, the parish was well established. As a youth, it was my pleasure and privilege to lead a choir of schoolboys in the small church. Our organist was Miss Beta Ekblom. Chief Altar boy for many years, indeed one could almost call him the unofficial curate, was Fergus O'Brien. Later still, in 1940, Father Campbell officiated at my wedding in our own church.

THE LYRIC AND THE MARKET

In Price Street was the "Lyric" cinema, known locally as the "Stagger in". Next to the Queens Pub, and opposite the Park entrance, was the Park Cinema, or "Saronys".

As "North enders", we seldom strayed beyond Duke Street, so the Park and Lyric cinemas were the haunts of "Townies", as anyone living on the other side of Duke Street was known.

It was not until schooldays were over that this world beyond our imaginary boundary came into its own. The magic era of Saturday nights at Birkenhead Market began. Stories about this wonderland of sights and extraordinary characters began to seep through. Thereafter Saturday nights were never the same without a long walk to Birkenhead Market. A tram ride from the depot at Mallaby Street/Laird Street, would have cost 1d each way. That 2d. could be used more enjoyably around the market.

The covered section comprised food, clothes and everyday goods stalls, and consequently a cursory walk through was usually afforded this section.

The real market, in our eyes, was outside on the paved area where such characters as "Bob Strong" sold his tonic. A comparable tonic today "fortifies the over forties." Bob stood, a living testimony to the efficacy of his potion. He was stripped to the waist in hail, rain or shine. I would say that he had a great physique. I would also guess that he would then be in his late forties.

Another regular Saturday nighter was O'Toole the Hair King who claimed to be able to grow hair on anything. Here again, coincidentally or no, he was living testimony to his product, having a thick mop of black hair and a huge moustache. My guess at O'Toole's age — mid-fifties to sixty.

A move across the setts now to the Lino man. He would stand on a platform, which was part of his open-sided lorry. The crowd would be shoulder to shoulder to about 6 yards around the back of his wagon and in front of him, his feet being about head level with his customers' heads. After a long, humorous spiel about his lino, ending in the usual, "Not £3, not £2 — here give me 30 bob for the lot." He would literally throw a roll of lino over the heads of the crowd to the screams of the ladies. For a split second it would form a ceiling overhead and then, just as swiftly, roll back to his arms. We could never understand how this miracle was achieved.

Up another line of stalls another wagon held miracle man number 2, the Pottery man. Here again there was the oft-repeated, but never boring, spiel, this time accompanied by an added plate or saucer to the collection on his arm. Our eyes would stand out like organ stops anticipating his adding one too many to the set on his arm and relishing the thought of the resulting crash. It never happened.

The cry of another character who could not pronounce his R's but who most certainly gave value for money, was "'ere Y'are, 6 cweam chocolates — 6 humbugs, 6 of this, 6 of that, and 'ere y'are, a cweamy whirl on top. All guawanteed pwoducts."

One permanent feature not to be omitted was the Whartons' goal, — two brothers, who alternated in goal, and the father who collected the penny or two pence a kick. The trick here, although few, if any, were aware of it because of the dim, flared light, was that a jet black board about a foot wide, ran around the inside of the white painted goal posts, thereby reducing the punters' chances by that much all around the posts. It was a good 'un who could collect his winnings, for, apart from the built-in handicap of the black boards, both the Wharton boys were experienced amateur goalkeepers for Shaftesbury Old Boys.

All of these characters, and more, made up a Saturday night's entertainment, equalled only by a night at the Argyle theatre. At the latter one had to pay, however, whereas the Market jaunts could result in a real bargain in addition to the entertainment provided by the stall holders.

HARRISON DRIVE

With age comes sophistication, in our case in the late '20s. The transition was from the childish acceptance of a bottle of water and a "butty" on Biddy Hill, to the teenage demand for recognition of our newly acquired status. The switch of venue was to the more glamorous Harrison Drive, or New Brighton.

It must seem inconceivable to today's youth, that if you were to arrive, pre-war, at that stretch of beach between the pier at New Brighton, to beyond Derby Pool at Harrison Drive, on a summer Sunday, after 10 a.m., you would have great difficulty in finding a spot to pitch a tent or to open a deck chair.

The steam trains would be packed to the doors. I have known the odd occasion when we were left at "Dock" Station, now Birkenhead North, unable to 'crush' in. The beach was clean, and whole families would disport themselves in a dozen different ways. Ball games would predominate. Inevitably the beach would have more than its share of youths exhibiting their physical prowess, mainly, I suspect, for the benefit of the bathing beauties.

However crowded the beach, the faithful and ever present string of donkeys would wend their way past the prone bodies of sunbathers, or youths in the "hand stand" position, without mishap to either.

After truly memorable hours, one was acutely aware that this vast crowd on the beach would be packing up ready for the journey home. If the trains to the beach were packed, spread over the morning, you can imagine Grove Road, Harrison Drive Station platform when the crowds converged upon it for departure. On one occasion I was terribly shocked to see a young girl fall between the platform and the running board of an incoming train. Fortunately the train had virtually stopped, but she was turned around two or three times by the running board before the end of the coach was reached and she dropped to the track. The crush was so great, indeed that had been the cause of her being pushed, that we were literally lifted involuntarily onto the train.

We were delayed for a time, all extremely concerned about the girl, but packed so tightly that it was impossible to ascertain the facts. Certain it was that restoration of the girl to the platform was the first consideration. We never did see the unfortunate girl, or even learn the extent of her injuries, if any.

Before leaving the events of these epic train journeys to Harrison Drive and New Brighton, I must mention that in contrast to the "faceless monsters" which now draw our trains, our steam locomotives were "personalised." Probably the most popular was the unofficially named "Lady Dean", whose driver was father to William Ralph "Dixie" Dean.

THE ONE O'CLOCK GUN

A sound so sadly missing nowadays is the boom of what was known as "The one o'clock gun."

The report from this ancient piece of musketry could be heard, literally, for miles around, and would produce an involuntary response from thousands of Merseysiders. This was a movement, in earlier days, to the waistcoat pocket, to check one's pocket watch, or, in later years, a flick of the jacket cuff, to expose a wrist watch.

The gun was as much a part of Merseyside life as the Liver birds, or the ferry boats. We, in Birkenhead, considered the gun to be our very own by virtue of the fact that it was sited on the Mersey wall near to the ferry and almost directly opposite to the Liver buildings on Liverpool's waterfront. An interesting point to make here, is that anyone standing on the Liverpool side of the river would hear the report just under four seconds after the actual firing.

The original gun, a 34-pounder from the Crimean war, was first fired on September 21st 1867 as a time check for ships in the river estuary and also for Merseyside chronometers.

The gun, which originally used seven pounds of powder, subsequently, after complaints of damage, reduced to 5 pounds, was in use until 1932.

On April 26th, 1933, a 32-pounder was brought up from Woolwich Arsenal which continued in service until September 1939. Firing was then discontinued for obvious reasons. Service was resumed in June 1946 to the delight of all.

Gun number 3 was a Hotchkiss 6-pounder, which continued the service until final withdrawal on July 18th 1969, so ending another era.

The guns were fired electronically from Bidston Observatory over 2-miles away, the Observatory taking its time directly from Greenwich.

The Observatory, around which as children we used to play, became world-famous in its own right during the Second World War. War time tides and times were plotted from this now vital link, for all major sea operations, including the very vital "D" day tides, so essential to the success of that vast undertaking.

Little did we "Blocks" children know, as we ran around this building, that in later years the skill of its operators, and the quality of its equipment, would play a leading role in an event the like of which the world had never known.

Chapter 6
THE END OF THE "BLOCKS"

There must have been many people who, on hearing that the old Blocks were to be demolished, felt, as I did, something akin to being informed that a very dear friend was doomed to die. It was to mean the loss of contact with so many dear friends and neighbours and to be left with just memories of a warmth of comradeship which I claim has not been equalled in any other community.

The Blocks were built 1844/47 — and were "murdered" 90 years later in 1937/40. It is significant and symptomatic of the times in which we live, that the replacement "Ilchester Gardens" lasted a mere handful of years.

A photograph of Alderman Chas McVey which appeared in the January 15th 1958 edition of our local paper showing the Alderman standing astride the remains of the old Blocks, 1939, bore the caption "To him it was a sad farewell to the property he has known since childhood, for was it not in one of these cottages, 60 years before, that he had been born."

There must have been many at that symbolic ceremony who echoed those sentiments a hundredfold.

Doubtless there will be those whose memory of the people and events about whom, and about which, I have presumed to write, will be at variance with mine. I can only hope that if this is so, at least the sincerity of my narrative will not be in doubt.

Each name, each place, each event, will I trust, evoke in the reader, as it did in me in its recall, waves of indescribable nostalgia which only a Dock cottager is privileged to enjoy.

In the first chapter of this booklet, various views are expressed as to the desirability of building blocks of flats.

Whatever the views of the "experts" and they had their own ideas of how the working class should live, my family moved into the "Blocks" and "Yours truly", the youngest of the Houldins, enjoyed the privilege of being one of a truly remarkable group of people among whom camaraderie was a byword.

My experience of being one of the "Blockites" is contained within this booklet and I would like to thank all those who have encouraged me to record my memories. I would also like to express my appreciation to Jean McInnes, Bill Norton and Ian Coles for their help with the publication of this booklet.